AF478486

Making Childhood Colorful

Designing Books for Children

Edited by Wang Xiaodan

Making Childhood Colorful

Designing Books for Children

images
Publishing

Contents

Making Childhood Colorful: Designing Books for Children

Children's books can entertain and educate children. Indeed, as children form an important segment of book readers, children's books form a significant category of book design. The content of children's books is intended to make children feel a sense of happiness, wonder, comfort, or adventure; provide them with fundamental, interesting, and constructive knowledge; and encourage their engagement with the content of a book both during and after the experience. As *Making Childhood Colorful: Designing Books for Children* demonstrates, creators of children's books–authors, illustrators, designers, and publishers–specifically target young readers with expressive, interactive, and distinctive designs that appeal to children's preferences, enrich their well-being, aid development, and fuel imagination.

Main Design Features of Children's Books

Children's cognitive and physical abilities, and aesthetic and storytelling preferences undoubtedly differ from adults and the successful design of children's books addresses these abilities and preferences. In addition, children's books are designed to arouse and maintain readers' interest for as long as possible. For these reasons, children's books predominantly feature expressive imagery, engaging formats, and recognizable characters in bright, muted, and monochromatic palettes. These elements appeal to children that, typically, are attracted to color, explore their environment through touch, and are familiar with images of animals and people.

Children typically mature mentally, psychologically, and physiologically as they grow, and children's books will vary for different levels of maturity. As such, the design of children's books should cater to the age and developmental level of the audience with artistry and text being simpler for younger children and more complex for older children.[1]

Children from three to five years of age learn by playing games and develop their senses through body movement, tactile sensation, and visual perception.[2] Thus, the design of children's books for this age group should be interactive and employ a variety of materials and images that enhance the perceptual experience.[3] In addition, although young children are interested in color they do not yet understand the concept of color, and it may be used subjectively and imaginatively to arouse interest rather than authentically portray the world.[4]

From six to eight years old is an important stage for children to gain knowledge and they establish a more intense need or desire to read books. Books designed for this school-age group can serve as a fundamental means of education as they convey information, facts, and concepts. More realistic use of color can enhance children's understanding.[5]

Children aged from nine to eleven years old acquire greater self-awareness and emotiveness and develop their own creative abilities and aesthetic preferences. Books for this age group should feature a strong graphic component, including more abstract illustrations, with a focus on emotional expression and creative forms. Lengthier texts can help children develop their thinking, reading, and comprehension skills.[6]

Imagery plays a very important part of children's books, particularly for children that have not yet mastered the skill of reading. Illustrations, fonts, colors, cover design, and layout are used to guide children's eyes across a page, helping them to follow the development of a story and stay focused on a book. This imagery can serve to express the plot, characters, and mood of a story and kindle children's interest and imagination.

The physical format and material composition of a book can stimulate children's senses and cognitive abilities as well as improving hand-eye coordination. Designers use a variety of techniques to encourage children to touch and feel different textures, fold and unfold pages, and pull and push tabs, amongst other interactive and tactile elements. With the goal to entertain and educate children, books may include additional activities such as puzzles, toys, stickers, games, and other supplements to engage children.

Children are drawn to cute and emotive objects and designers will endow story characters with these qualities. Children are also drawn to characters and objects in books that are familiar and recognizable and consistent with their own surroundings or knowledge. As such, authors and designers will frequently include animals and people in stories and illustrations, giving them expressive and emotive faces and behavior. By featuring animals and/or people in a story, books can blur the lines between imagination and reality for children.

Overall, the design of children's books is intended to encourage children to follow a story; learn and understand letters, numbers, language, concepts, and emotions; stimulate their imagination; and help them make sense of the world in which they live.

Design Categories of Children's Books

Analysis of the case studies suggests children's books can be broadly divided into categories that include popular science, education, enlightenment, literature, cartoon, and handcraft books, plus more. Three main classifications of the design of children's books are picture books, pop-up books, and interactive books. These categories address children's cognitive abilities and physical senses.

1. Picture Books

Picture books tell a story through illustrations and images. As the name suggests, pictures dominate the content of picture books—rather than being an adjunct to text—and are designed to help children understand and follow the narrative and characters of a story without having to read text. For this reason, some picture books are wordless while others include short texts, which can help young children learn to read. Both multi-color and black-and-white picture books are intended to engage children and in some cases the images in these books can be appreciated as artworks on their own.

Picture books have existed for hundreds of years in some form. *Orbis Pictus*, by famous Czech educator Johann Amos Comenius and first published in 1658, is one of the first picture books intended for children. It is a primary school Latin textbook based on the author's theories of approaching learning based on the principles of nature and it introduces 24 letters with various animal sounds.[7] *Orbis Pictus* has 150 short articles accompanied by illustrations related to nature (e.g., the universe, geography, plants, animals, and human bodies), human activities (e.g., agriculture, handcraft, transportation, and culture), social life (national administrations and courts), and language, plus others, with the aim to convey encyclopedic knowledge to children. Used in schools across Europe, the book has had a great influence on both western textbooks and children's books. Picture books have evolved over time and designers will sometimes adopt a style that references features of historic picture books. Picture books come in different sizes (e.g., 8vo, 12mo, 48mo, and 64mo) and with different bindings, such as hardcover, paperback, and cardboard.

Young children have a better understanding of pictures than words because their mental capacity is still maturing. As such, the imagery in picture books has a more narrative nature and function than

other categories of children's books because the visual aspect is easier for children to understand. Children learn a visual language—including images, pictures, people, objects, and spaces—before a verbal language, and for the first years of a child's life their interest in pictures outweighs their interest in text because it is a language they can comprehend. As they learn to understand letters and read words, short lines of text can guide children's understanding of a story. However, pictures continue to be very important as they can reveal character emotions and plot elements that can't be clearly expressed in words appropriate for the audience's reading level.

'About Lamb' (Fig. 1) tells the story of a lonely lamb traveling the world to find friends. The mixed-media illustrations are made using acrylic paint and newspaper collage. The designer Daria Maksimova believes in a minimalist approach and that a story should be presented visually and understood easily, even without words. Thus, the designer's illustrations are intended to speak for themselves with no unnecessary elements or detail. The book has a simple red, blue, and yellow color palette, and text is included only as a supplement.

By definition, pictures are the principle part of children's picture books while texts are complementary. The interdependence of imagery, as well as the relation of texts to images, will influence both the layout of a page or book and how a story is conveyed to readers. Designers arrange the content of a book so the front cover, flyleaf, pictures, texts, and back cover are unified and coherent. This layout influences the style and overall feel of a book and is designed to address children's preferences in order to attract their interest and affection, and to look recognizable and feel familiar.

2. Pop-up Books

A pop-up book, also called a movable book, can be considered both a book and a toy as it has the content and form of a book combined with the interactive nature of a toy. Pop-up books are an art form that requires designers to adapt and transform the content of a story into two-or three-dimensional structural features. For example, opening or turning a page in a pop-up book will activate applied elements that transform into three-dimensional images. Other interactive tricks include wheels to turn, pages to fold, and tabs to lift, revealing and obscuring pictures and texts.

The concept of pop-up books first emerged in the thirteenth century when British friars added revolving discs to books and in 1765, British publisher Robert Sayer produced the first series of movable toy books for children. A golden age of pop-up books came in the 1800s when publishers created books to foster reading among children, and by 1860 movable books were being produced on a mass scale. Blue Ribbon Publishing of New York coined the phrase 'pop-up book' in the 1930s when it produced a series of movable picture books that animated Walt Disney characters and fairy tales. Since then, the forms of pop-up books have continued to progress with innovations in paper engineering and creative design.[8]

Pop-up books are intended to surprise and fascinate children. They challenge children's expectations, stimulate curiosity, and offer new experiences while encouraging them to observe, touch, and think about the dimensionality or structure of an image. These interesting and often intriguing features can be helpful in developing children's reading habits as children want to explore these books time and time again.

The transformative nature of a pop-up book is attractive to children. Moving elements that require children to touch, turn, discover, fold, open, close, and extend can engage curiosity and focus attention. They can also help children to more vividly understand a story, expounding the themes, characters, and plot by virtue of transforming flat pictures into two- or three-dimensional images. These interactive features cater to children's desire to touch and explore objects with their hands, and operating individual elements can help them use their hands in defined movements.Ultimately, this process of operation can aid the development of fine motor skills and dexterity, build muscle control, improve hand-eye coordination, and encourage problem solving and other cognitive and physical development.

Common pop-up books can be divided into pull-tabs, pop-outs, and toy books. In a pull-tab book, an applied element can be horizontally or vertically separated from the rest of a page by sliding, pulling, lifting, or pushing. Pop-outs are revealed in a variety of creative and inventive layouts and arrangements,

and are flat when a book or page is closed, but three-dimensional when a book or page is open.

Bobropediya (Fig. 2) is a pop-up book designed for children of BBR Bank's clients to increase brand loyalty and promote positive feelings toward the bank. This book has nine spreads that retell classic stories in a humorous way and each spread has an illustration and pop-out image accompanied by a poem or text. *Bobropediya* is square in shape and made with paper and cardboard with gloss varnish and matte laminate. Brightly colored three-dimensional illusions pop-out whenever a page is turned, presenting the content of the book in an interesting and stereoscopic way.

Pop-out books with two- and three-dimensional effects can stoke children's curiosity and imagination as well as providing images that may more closely reflect the real world. By encouraging visual observation and tactile exploration, the novel and interactive forms of pop-up books can stimulate children's desire to read and engage with books.

3. Interactive Books

Interactive books encourage children's active participation in the content of a book. They are designed to entertain and educate children through an experience that combines reading with games and activities. While the nature of these books reflects the increasing interactivity of modern technology, as tangible objects they continue to help children be familiar and comfortable with books and reading.

The history of interactive books is closely related with pop-up books, providing children with more physically engaging material. The development of computers and Internet technology has modified the

Designer
Devi Soewono

Size
210mm x 210mm x
10mm

Completion
2012

design and content possibilities of interactive books as well as changing reading habits.[9]

'How to Draw Birds of Indonesia' (Fig. 3) by Devi Soewono is a three-book series, contained in a carry case, intended to foster greater appreciation of

endangered Indonesian bird species. Soewono aims to increase children's awareness and knowledge by teaching readers how to draw local birds. Visually, bright yellow illustrations stand out against a dark gray background with light gray texts.

The intricate and detailed formats of interactive books require children to be more intimately and actively involved and the simplicity or complexity of these formats is intended to suit children's level of development and cognitive capabilities. The pop-up book is also a type of interactive book, however, it features strong graphic form rather than games and activities.

Materials are an important element of the design of interactive books. Different materials offer different tactile experiences and can be used to encourage children to explore the content of a book, enhancing their tactile perception. The selection of materials should feel good to children and may include fabric, plastic, paper, or other textured and appropriate materials. Interactive toy books can emit sounds or scents that stimulate children's auditory and olfactory systems, and incorporate tools (e.g., mirrors, convex lens panels, and fluorescent ink) that provide interesting visual effects.

Luisa Zamora's interactive book 'Darkness Can Also Be Fun' (*La Oscuridad También Puede Ser Divertida*) (Fig. 4) is designed for children over four years of age and aims to help them develop their fine motor skills and overcome their fear of the dark. It is made from cardboard, artificial leather, adhesive paper, printed fabric, and gloss varnish and encourages children to use their hands to complete various activities such as sticking ties and buttons to illustrations. Children can do the activities on their own or with

3

assistance and gain active, hands-on experience through immersive participation.

Coloring-in books offer another kind of interactive activity and can help children develop their understanding of colors, including the objective and psychological properties of colors. As children add color to line art—using crayons, colored pencils, and marker pens—they learn to identify images, use color imaginatively, and develop hand-eye coordination and fine motor skills.

The design of interactive books is closely aligned with philosopher and psychologist John Dewey's theory that a child's instincts, activities, and interests should form the start of their education and be developed by their own abilities.[10] Thus, interactive books are a tool that can be used to educate children (often without them realizing) while also entertaining and occupying their attention.

Applying the Art of Design to Children's Books

1. Illustration Design

Illustration design is an important part of children's books and children are typically attracted to vivid illustrations. As a substitute for words, illustrations can represent an entire story and in some cases, particularly for those not yet able to read, children's understanding of a book will depend solely on pictures. Illustrated books should be appropriate for children's level of development while expressive graphics can arouse children's interest, cultivate imagination, and stimulate creativity.

Imagination is the basis of illustration in the design of children's books. Vibrant images help encourage

5

children's imagination and may be influential to the point that children might imagine characters and stories as part of their life. Thus, as children live in both the real world and their own imagined worlds, and find pleasure in things that may seem insignificant to adults, illustrations can help inspire children's own imagination and creativity.

Hyperbole and personification are commonly used in children's book illustrations as designers create images with exaggerated forms and emotive expressions. Illustrators must use their own imagination to create stimulating illustrations as well as to depict plots and characters that cannot happen or do not exist in real life.

Successful illustration design in children's books is not limited to storytelling, but can also convey facts; natural, cultural, or scientific information; plus more. Children gain education and entertainment from visual information, which can challenge their thinking and offer new visual and cognitive experiences.

Graphic illustrations are one of the most visually comprehendible languages for children. Young children lack the concept of space and perspective and perceive objects as planar. Thus, two-dimensional illustrations are easier for them to understand and can decrease the difficulty of identifying objects.

The diversity of techniques, themes, and styles of illustrations in children's books offer a rich visual experience. Illustrative techniques include painting, drawing, cutting, sticking, carving, molding, and digital editing. Designers incorporate broad themes, such as nature, science, humanity, and fantasy, into illustrations. Furthermore, national or regional styles of art and culture can be integrated into illustrations to convey information about a particular area while teaching children about their native land or other countries from an early age.

In 'Tales by Borys Grinchenko' (Fig. 5), designer Oksana Fedko uses a collage of illustrations and embroidery—a traditional Ukrainian folk art—to cultivate children's interest in Ukrainian culture, folklore, and folk art. The designer photographed their grandmother's embroidered pieces and processed the photos using graphic-editing software. The embroidered elements are set atop a canvas background and combined with illustrations to reveal the nature and symbolism of the fairy tale plot and to depict characters in Ukrainian national dress.

2. Font Design

Letters, characters, and symbols are mainly used to convey information, and typeface selection will determine their readability and appearance. Fonts in varying styles and sizes can be used to help express the feeling, meaning, or content of words. Graphic and expressive fonts are a common feature in the design of children's books and the variety of font designs can stimulate children's imagination, enrich their reading experience, and help them better understand the content of a book.

Style and size are two of the main characteristics of font design. Designers choose fonts in which the style and size is, first and foremost, readable and legible, and secondly, effective in the layout of the book. The font size in children's books should be of reasonable size for children to identify letters and numbers and read words and sentences. Font size should cater to children's developmental level in order to help them establish good reading habits and contribute to the healthy maturation of their

eyesight. This is particularly important for young children, as fonts that are too large or too small can be an obstacle to reading or vision development.

While designers employ diverse typefaces and font styles they also create their own freehand illustrative typography to express a lively and child-like aesthetic. Designers use a variety of drawing tools (e.g., colored pencils, fountain pens, writing brushes, charcoal pencils, and crayons) and techniques (e.g., sticking, rubbing, and paper cutting) to make texts appear more visually meaningful and interesting. Computer fonts are generally simpler than handwritten typography and clear and interesting fonts on book covers can encourage children to take a closer look.

Lady René (Fig. 6) is a typography catalog that presents designer and illustrator Laura Varsky's

lettering work. The narrative is based on the popular late-nineteenth century American song "The Cat Came Back," written by Harry S. Miller, and the book has a final dossier that teaches children what a font is and how fonts are classified. Readers are invited to draw their own fonts at the end of the book. Varsky's typeface is fluid and flexible with a strong decorative effect. The designer integrates texts into illustrations for a highly graphic result intended to appeal to children.

An underlying principle of font selection and design in children's books is the need for them to be visually simple and clear to read. Font style, size, color, and letter spacing can be used to help children identify letters, symbols, and words, and understand their meanings. Size and spacing should be appropriate for the reading level of children; for example, larger letters and expanded spaces can help children read. Furthermore, as text color is not confined to black, and ensuring that color does not affect readability, a large variety of colors can be used to complement or contrast texts with images and background. In all, the selection of typeface and font style, color, and size can enhance a book's ability to attract and maintain children's attention.

3. Color Design

Children are, in general, attracted to bright colors and they may choose a book solely for its color. In addition, children do not always perceive colors objectively; that is to say, the sky might not be always blue, trees not always green, and the sun not always yellow. Therefore, when choosing colors for a children's book, designers should appeal to children's imaginative preferences, aid their ability to identify and associate colors, and choose colors that complement the content of a book.

Color serves as a silent book salesman and designers and publishers use color to help a children's book stand out from numerous other children's books. Furthermore, the color of a book's cover should speak to children's naive and curious nature with vivid or various colors.

Designers can choose colors according to children's psychological and physiological factors and aesthetic preferences. Generally speaking, very young children can recognize primary colors and learn to establish the relationship between basic colors and their names; at four or five years of age, children can identify a greater variety of colors and have their own favorite colors; and children six years old and over have more capacity to identify colors and use colors objectively. Color choice can also be based on appealing to different age groups and genders of children. For example, some designers may employ different colors to appeal to boys or girls, or have two versions of a book in which one color palette is intended for younger children and another color palette for older children.

Bright and brilliant colors have a strong visual impact and children's books will often have vividly contrasting colors. However, designers should not use bright colors just for the sake of it; rather, they should choose a color palette that complements the content of a book and appeals to children's preferences. As they age, children's fondness for intense and saturated colors can change and they begin to develop their own color preferences. For example, some children like warm colors, such as red and yellow, and some prefer cold colors, such as blue. Thus, designers should adjust colors appropriately for children's ages and preferences and achieve color balance by neutralizing bright colors with black, white, and gray.

Я сутки напролет сидел да ел, ел да пил, ел не толь-ко досыта — ел до устали.

Как платить запонадобилось, я месяцем сосветил и на поезд пошел. В вагон не полез: в вагоне с месяцем тесно, да никто не увидит моей нарядности. Сел я на платформу. Меня подушками обложили. Шинель я снял. Ну и сияние пошло! Это для неба месяц был не гож да прошломесячной, а для нас дак очень даже светел.

Светило не с неба на землю, а с земли до неба, и така была светлая ясность, что всю дорогу встречали, провожали с музыкой и пели: «Светит месяц».

Только вот месяц на небе в холоду держался да ветром обдувался, а здесь на земле тухнуть стал — и погас.

В хозяйстве все в дело идет. На том месяце наши хозяйки блины пекут. Как сковородка месяц и великоват, ну да большому куску рот радуется.

В гости приходи — блинами угостим: блины-то каждый с месяц ростом, поешь — верить станешь.

20

7

In 'Don't Like It–Don't Listen' (FIg. 7), designer Rita Chcrcpanova lookcd at Russian folktalcs through the eyes of a modern city girl to demonstrate how folk art can be fresh and interesting. The result is a book that mixes a graphic novel with a traditional tale. 'Real world' illustrations are in black gouache and 'fairy tale' illustrations in cyan, pink, and yellow for a contemporary yet vintage feeling.

Color is one of the most important factors in children's book design and particular colors will not only attract children to a book but also suggest the mood of a book. Thus, the design of a children's book should suit its content by using colors that correspond.

4. Layout Design

Layout design refers to the arrangement of illustrations and texts and the creation of a unified design. Layout can enrich both the aesthetic and readability of a book and therefore designers should fully consider the relationship between illustrative and text elements. Designers should also layout a book in accord with its specific content, positioning titles, texts, headings, and other elements in an ordered and comprehendible fashion for children to follow and understand.

Layouts commonly used in children's books include landscape, portrait, free, cross, diagonal, and triangle, which can also be classified according to line type, being divided into unidirectional lines, bidirectional lines, radial lines, and curves. More rigid layouts can guide children's eyes across the page and help them to understand the development of a story, while freer and more expressive layouts tend to add visual interest to a book.

Children are better able to recognize images than texts and designers will not directly place long paragraphs on top of pictures. Rather, a free layout, with pictures arranged loosely and without

any rigorous structure, will commonly integrate graphics and texts, making words part of pictures. In contrast, in more structured layouts, in which graphics and texts are relatively independent of each other, designers will position texts and graphics so as not to sacrifice readability or clarity.

In 'Words to the Point' (Fig. 8), Monika Grubizna explains the meaning of classic Polish proverbs and phrases. Each illustration depicts an object in the collection of the Ethnographic Museum in Kraków and is accompanied by the meaning of the relevant proverb. Grubizna employs a free layout and combines descriptive texts with pictures, and takes advantage of white space and background colors to separate texts from illustrations. The book is laid out in alphabetical order and the back cover provides a space for children's activities, such as drawing objects, making notes, and writing letters. The book is intended to bring children and adults together to read and share their knowledge and experience.

Overall, layout can be used to convey the content of a story, make books more visually powerful, and appeal to children.

5. Cover Design

A book cover is designed to reflect a book's content and be a selling point both in influencing purchase and encouraging children to read it. Image, text, and color are three basic elements of cover design that designers combine to convey information and create a visual aesthetic for a book.

The cover design of children's books is intended to be creative, interesting, expressive, and eye-catching, and simple, clear covers with bright colors are more likely to attract children's attention quickly. In general, children aged from six to eight years old are curious and keen to learn and the design of book covers for these children should simply and directly highlight the knowledge readers can gain. Children nine years of age and older begin to develop their own modes of thinking and the design of book covers for this age group should be more artistic, employing both complex and rational design approaches to increase children's understanding of aesthetics.

Pictures form a main element of book covers because images have a strong visual impact and resonance with young children. Images that reflect the main content of a book can help children more quickly understand that content. Common subjects of illustrations include figures, animals, cartoons, landscapes, and plants, and they are designed to take up large amounts of space to create a visual impression. Cover text is composed of the book's title and author and publisher names. In addition, color should reflect the content of a book and can be used to attract children's attention.

The paper or material used for a book cover is generally thicker than the leaves of a book as it needs to protect the pages and be easy for readers to hold and store. Covers may also be made from other durable materials, such as cotton, foam, cardboard, and plastic.

6. Physical Format Design

Physical format is the size and binding of the individual leaves in a book. Traditionally, the common size has been 16mo and 32mo, but due to the development and evolution of book design and production, many children's books have a unique physical format. Thus, there is no fixed size in today's children's books.

The format of a book can be used to spark children's interest and colorful, changeable, novel, and decorative forms can capture attention. Some of these formats break the traditional rectangle and are shaped like animals, plants, and characters to inspire children's curiosity. Decoration can be used to indicate the content of a book or story and contribute charm to the aesthetic of a book.

'Octopuses of a Same Tentacle Flock Together' (*Cada Pulpo Con Su Pulpa*) (Fig. 9) is a folded accordion book in which readers can discover odd pairs of connected animals. Marco Guardiola used one double sided sheet of paper (approximately

10

40cm by 40cm) cut to a spiral format. As children turn the book to read the story the animal body and texts run across each fold.

7. Material Design

The material composition of a book contributes to its tactile and visual effect. The various properties of materials—texture, color, and transparency—can stimulate different sensory, visual, and cognitive experiences. For example, rough or delicate, smooth or textured, and heavy or light materials will all look and feel different. In addition, materials form an expressive design language that, like graphics and texts, can be used to convey narrative, characters, and other information.

Although the design of children's books is varied, paper is the most common material as paper books are easier to produce and as such are more reasonably priced. Fabric, such as cotton and linen, is also popular for children's books—particularly those intended for younger children—as the material is durable, safe, and tougher and thicker than paper. Fabric books feel warm and comfortable in children's hands and are generally better for the environment than paper books. Plastic is a light and flexible material that can be used for the cover of children's books and designers employ a variety of

techniques to create decorative surface patterns. Elena Khodatska's 'Children's Quiet Book' (Fig. 10) is for children aged one year old and over, and it is made of cloth that is soft to the touch and can't be torn. Different clasps on each page include buttons, knobs, shoelaces, zippers, pins, and yarn, which encourage children to feel the book and develop the use of their hands.

Designers will also combine a number of different materials to create varied tactile experiences, and the successful design of a children's book will fully consider children's sensory abilities and experiences.

Design Trends

1. Interactivity

Designers should first consider the age group the book is intended for and not limit design to the style and format of traditional books. Rather they should pay attention to how children interact with books, for example, touching buttons that make sounds, pulling tabs that activate two-dimensional moving effects, and using other features that can emit scents.

Interactive features can intensify children's sensory, cognitive, and emotional experience of a book and may lay the basis of future trends in the development of the design of children's books. As multimedia technology advances, children's books should tend towards incorporating various and numerous media platforms, such as paper books, e-books, phones, tablets, and PCs.

Interactive children's books will most likely become increasingly high-tech and electronic reading machines and reading pens can be used to help children learn to read. In recent years, publishers have attempted to unite traditional books with innovative technology, such as Augmented Reality (AR), to make static pictures and texts more dynamic and to enrich the interactive experience of a book. AR is based on virtual reality and, able to present the content of a book in three-dimensional form, overturns the traditional reading experience. It superimposes visual images over real scenes in real time to create an interactive world on the phone, computer, or tablet screen that blurs the lines between virtual and real. At this stage, publishers exploring AR have only applied the technology to limited pages due to the high cost of programming development and production. However, while still at the explorative phase, the application of AR could well be a trend in the future design of children's books.

2. Interestingness

Interestingness is the power to attract and hold attention. In regard to the design of children's books interestingness is the power to captivate young readers' attention by appealing to their curiosity, imagination, and desire to learn. German aesthetician Johann Christoph Friedrich von Schiller in his prose *On the Aesthetic Education of Man* proposed that even the greatest talent must sacrifice their supreme authority for interestingness.[11]

As reading can form a part of playing for children, an important goal of the design of children's books is to incite pleasure in young readers. Imagery of animals, people, flowers, and other subjects can add to the interestingness of a book. Furthermore, diverse materials, sound buttons, three-dimensional illusions, and interactive activities can enhance the interestingness of a book and encourage children to view books like games, stimulating them to read, imagine, and create.

Designers can employ interactive features and different formats as a substitute for abstract concepts, which are more difficult for children to understand. Children like to repeat actions such as folding, pushing, and turning, and designers should structure a book to encourage and satisfy these behavioral tendencies.

3. Experience

Children can derive pleasure from participating in experiential games. Friedrich Froebel, a famous German educator, theorized that activities aid in the development of a child's nature and that games are a main form of recreational and educational activity for young children.[12]

Interactive books can intensify children's experience. Format, layout, and activities, such as paper folding, puzzles, mazes, connecting numbers, and painting, can encourage children to peruse a book and complete tasks alone or with parents and playmates. Supplementary items, such as stickers, can increase children's interaction with books, improve their fine motor skills, and develop their creativity, thinking, and patience. Freebies, such as a pack of seeds, can also be used to enrich the content of a book. For example, children can read a book to learn about plants and then sow the seeds in real life.

The design of children's books should address the full sensory experience. For example, pop-up books should go beyond being only visual and have sounds, textures, and scents. Touch is one of the main senses that young children use to understand the world and paper pages can be easily ripped, potentially reducing the physical lifespan of a book. While most children's books use coated paper, there is now a large number with pages that cannot be torn. Designers use fabric, such as cotton, which is soft, light, non-toxic, environmentally friendly, and easy to clean, to increase the durability of a book.

Children acquire knowledge by diverse methods and sources, which impact the role of traditional books. In this age of multimedia and multi-layered experience children have become accustomed to intense external sensory stimulation, and interactivity, interestingness, and experience have become vital aspects of the successful design of children's books. Therefore, the future design of children's books should cater to all five senses and fully consider children's psychological and physiological development to deepen children's engagement with books. This will serve to enrich the pleasurable experience children derive from books and develop their ability to imagine and create. Furthermore, the design of children's books should encourage children to read (rather than listen) and fully and actively participate in the content of a book to enhance the emotional, physical, and cognitive experience.

References

1. Elliot W. Eisner, *Development of Children's Perception and Vision*, trans. Sun Hong (Hunan: Hunan Fine Arts Publishing House, 1996), 111.

2. Victor Lowenfeld, *Creative and Mental Growth*, trans. Wang Deyu (Hunan: Hunan Fine Arts Publishing House, 1993), 101.

3. Lv Jingren, *Book Design Courses* (Hubei: Hubei Fine Arts Publishing House, 2006), 111.

4. Lowenfeld, *Creative and Mental Growth*, 114.

5. Lowenfeld, *Creative and Mental Growth*, 152.

6. Lowenfeld, *Creative and Mental Growth*, 178.

7. Zhang Daosen, *Zhongwai Meishu Jiaoyushi* (Beijing: China Social Sciences Press, 2011), 101.

8. Wu Jianyi, *History of Books* (Shanxi: Hope Publishing House, 2008).

9. Wu Jianyi, *History of Books* (Shanxi: Hope Publishing House, 2008).

10. Zhang Daosen, *Zhongwai Meishu Jiaoyushi*, 218-19.

11. Johann Christoph Friedrich von Schiller, *On the Aesthetic Education of Man*, trans. Xu Hengchun (Beijing: China Federation of Literary and Art, 1984).

12. Zhang Daosen, *Zhongwai Meishu Jiaoyushi*, 130-31.

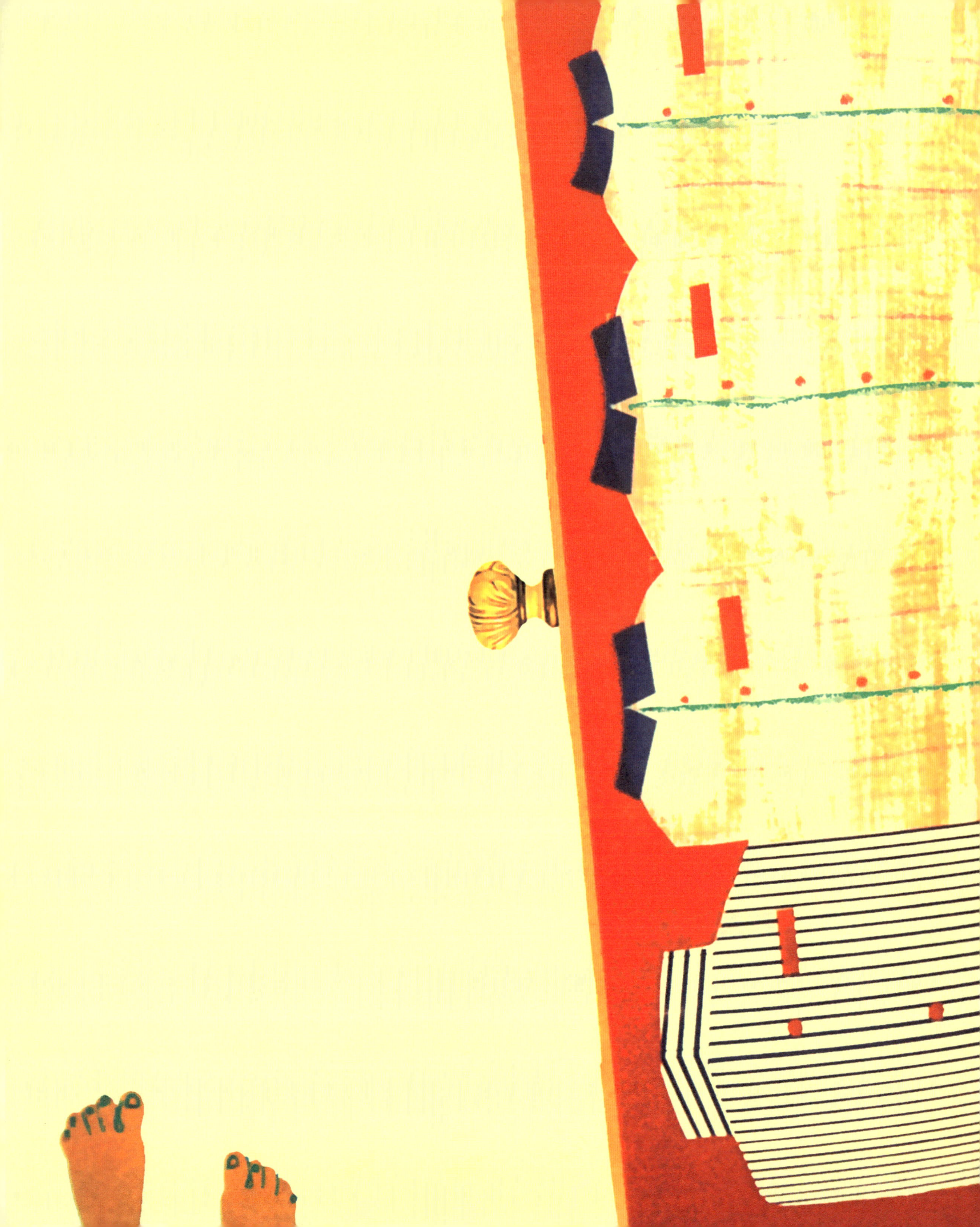

Picture Books

Norse Mythology Monsters Guide

Designer
Pierre Kleinhouse

Size
300mm x 300mm

Completion
2015

Pierre Kleinhouse created a fun and colorful book to present Norse mythology to children. The cover features one of the designer's favorite Norse mythology monsters—an enormous octopus Kraken—and each spread introduces a different monster, such as the wolf Fenrir, dragon Nidhogg, and snake Jormungandr.

The designer tried to make the monsters appear large within the compositions, without being too scary. In contrast to the designer's illustrations that are usually clean and vector-like, in this project Kleinhouse developed a fun and looser, freer style by using different brushes and textures.

סְקוֹל וְהָאָתִי הם בניו של פֶנְרִיר הזאב המפלצתי. סְקוֹל רודף אחרי השמש וְהָאָתִי אחרי הירח וכך הם גורמים להם לנוע סביב העולם. אולי יום אחד הם יתפסו ויזללו אותם!

נִירהוֹג הוא דרקון רשע הח...
ייגדְרָאסִיל שמחזיק את העולם...
בתקווה שיום אחד יצליח להפ...

יוֹרמוּנגָאנְדְר הנחש הוא בנו של האל לוקי והענקית אַנְגְרְבוֹדָה, אחיו הם פֶנְרִיר הזאב והאלה הֵל. הוא הוטל לתוך הים המקיף את מִידגָארְד, עולם בני האדם. גודלו נעשה כה עצום עד כי הוא נאלץ לנשוך את זנבו.

פָאפְנִיר היה גמד חמדן שרצה לשמור על האוצר של מִלְוואלִי לעצמו, אך האוצר היה מקולל והפך אותו לדרקון. מאז, הוא שומר בקנאות על האוצר ומבריח את אויביו בעזרת הבל הפה הרעיל שלו.

The Mystery of a Palm Syrup

Designer
Sasha Dolzhnitskaya

Material
Appliqué, collage, digital art

Printing Technology
Matte lamination

Size
250mm x 250mm

Completion
2014

'The Mystery of Palm Syrup' (*Moustaches Ungirdled*) is a two-part book that tells a story about an English gentleman and his out-of-control moustache. The first part of the book is brightly colored and features the animated adventures of the characters. The second part is the narrator's diary, illustrated in one color to provide coloring-in activities for readers. Sasha Dolzhnitskaya wrote the text freehand to create the feeling of a diary. Each leaf has a different composition and a variety of image angles. Dolzhnitskaya used mixed-media techniques to create the illustrations—finished in Photoshop—by combining magazine collage, colored paper, and tracing paper.

вскружила голову полисмену, и совсем запуталась в себе. Ох уж эта Молли Полли!

– Милый Оливер! – Взмолилась Молли Полли – Что же нам теперь делать? Мы все запутались!

«И впрямь, они все запутались…» - подумал Оливер и от отчаяния у него даже задрожали губы.

Оливер никогда не был плаксой, но он так привык полагаться во всем на свою драгоценную Молли Полли, что совсем расстроился и пал духом.

– Бедные мы бедные! – всхлипнул сосед Бобби. – Самим нам теперь точно не выпутаться! Если кто и поможет нам теперь, то только мадам Гала! Уж она-то знает толк в усах…

В чем же знала толк мадам Гала?

Б Больше всего на свете мадам Гала знала толк в кроликах и речной рыбе, и каждую осень, если конечно та выдавалась теплой, гостила в деревне у Бобби. Она водила с ним знакомство, еще с тех незапамятных времен, когда лечилась от туберкулеза в санатории, где тот, в дни разудалой молодости

44

О Ох уж эта Молли Полли! А как же зачекательная история, когда Оливер никак не мог решить какие туфли ему надеть, коричневые с пряжками или тоже коричневые, но без? Он пол дня не мог выйти на прогулку, сомневаясь, в каких туфлях ему идти. Находчивая Молли Полли отпорола пряжки с коричневых туфлей и пришила на свои новые сапожки!

В общем, Оливер мог положиться на Молли Полли во всем, и даже собирался жениться на ней, но все никак не мог собраться. Кроме того, будучи его домработницей, она никогда не позволяла себе фривольностей и всегда подолгу очень серьезно смотрела ему в глаза, когда он делал попытки класть руку ниже чем следовало лепить это джентльмену.

21

му тоже являются чертой отрицательной. Увидев Молли Полли, дядюшка Честер по обыкновению разразился добродушными проклятиями, а Оливер, как и полагается джентльмену, остался немногословен и предусмотрительно, опасаясь за свои чудесные нос и уши, предоставил слово Молли Полли.

– Дорогой дядюшка, – прощебетала Молли Полли – представь себе; у нас пикантный, что ни говори, вопрос встал вдруг на повестке дня! У нас... – Молли Полли понизила голос и наклонилась поближе к дядюшке – У нас пошли вразнос усы! – и, обернувшись, она обнадеживающе улыбнулась Оливеру своей самой заботливой улыбкой. Усы у Оливера встревоженно затрещали и встали дыбом, лишь только речь зашла об их утренних бесчинствах. Молли Полли подвела дядю Честера поближе, чтобы тот смог рассмотреть сию пикантную причину и указала на нее пальцем. – Вот! Распоясались!

Дядя Честер был немало удивлен и обескуражен подобным поведением усов, ведь его усища были много старше и никогда не позволяли себе подобного, а тут – на тебе! Бардак!

– Ну, знаете ли, это ни в какие ворота не лезет! Усы усами, но такое – немыслимо просто! Столько лет но

33

по закашлялся – У меня где-то завалялись отменные усы... Ах, вот же они! – дядя Честер показался в дверях своего кабинета с размашистыми пиратскими усами в руках.

Оливер скоро перебрал по памяти все свои щегольские наряды и представил их в только наметившимся соседстве с пиратскими усищами. От сего гротескного натюрморта, написанного потрясенным воображением у него закружилась голова и немножечко потемнело в глазах. Ощутив слабость в ногах он схватился рукой за дверной косяк и прижался к нему щекой. «Однако же, что за напасть с этими усами!» – подумал Оливер – «Что ни новость, то расстройство...», и обреченно протянул руку за новыми усами.

Как же пришились Оливеру новые усы?

– Замечательно пришлись! – Сказала Молли Полли и закусила губу. А дядя Честер не удержался и даже чмокнул Оливера в щеку, так он рад был его новым пиратским усам. Пышные, бархатистые, изящные усы гордо обрамляли нежные щеки своего нового владельца, добавляя мужественности и стати. И даже старые усы Оливера заходили ходуном от восхищения, шурша и потрескивая, да так, что дядюшка Честер с трудом мог удержать их.

Краснея и смущаясь, Оливер оглядывал себя и свои новые усища в зер

Мадам Гала, от души довольная исполненным ею номером, пригласила всех отужинать. Она прожарила усы так, что они превратились в рыбу, и накрыла на стол. Рыба получилась отменная, жаль, только, по-настоящему могла оценить ее лишь одна мадам Гала, да, пожалуй, кот Мопис, которому, впрочем, тоже очень понравилось.

60

Что же предпринял дядюшка Честер?

Дядюшка Честер был старым морским волком, и на своей памяти брился только в день совершеннолетия своей племянницы – Молли Полли, и в усах, как и бороде он явно знал толк. Мечтая о военной карьере для своей обожаемой родственницы, дядюшка Честер не жалел ни времени, ни сил, чтобы привить ей черты самые важные для человека военного: находчивость и непоколебимость, ибо находчивый не потеряется по определению, а колебания плохо сказываются на пищеварении, посе-

30

29

Little Zaches

Author
E.T.A. Hoffman

Designer
Yulia Khokhlova

Material
Paper, collage

Size
210mm x 270mm

Completion
2013

Yulia Khokhlova illustrated 'Little Zaches,' one of E.T.A. Hoffmann's bright and magical novels about an evil dwarf, beautiful love, kind fairies, and cunning wizards. The designer used collage for illustrations; colored pencils, colored paper, and fabric for pictures; and added magazine clippings for a more realistic feeling. Illustrations and pictures are combined with text for an interesting, lively, and harmonious book.

щие стрекозьи крылья были у нее за плечами, белые и красные розы заплетены в волосах. «Эге-ге!» — прошептал Проспер, спрятав трость под шлафрок, и тотчас дама предстала в прежнем своем виде.

Проспер Альпанус приветливо пригласил ее сесть. Фрейлейн фон Розеншён сказала, что у нее было давнишнее намерение посетить господина доктора в его сельском доме, дабы приобрести знакомство с человеком, коего вся округа славит как весьма искусного, благодетельного мудреца. Верно, он удовольствует ее просьбу и согласится как врач наблюдать за расположенным неподалеку приютом для благородных девиц, ибо старые дамы частенько прихварывают и не получают никакой помощи. Проспер Альпанус учтиво ответил, что хотя он уже давно оставил практику, но согласен сделать исключение и в случае надобности посетить призреваемых девиц, затем он осведомился, не страдает ли сама фрейлейн фон Розеншён от какого-нибудь недуга. Фрейлейн ответила уверением, что она лишь время от времени замечает ревматические боли в членах, когда ей случается простудиться на утренней прогулке, но сейчас она совершенно здорова, и тут она перевела беседу на какую-то безразличную тему. Проспер спросил, не желает ли она, так как только что наступило утро, выпить чашку кофе? Розеншён заметила, что канониссы никогда не пренебрегают этим. Кофе подали, но, как ни старался Проспер налить его, чашки оставались пустыми, хотя кофе и лилось из кофейника.

— Э-э! — улыбнулся Проспер Альпанус. — Да это строптивый кофе! Не угодно ли вам, досточтимая фрейлейн, разлить самой?

— С удовольствием, — отвечала фрейлейн и взяла кофейник. Но, несмотря на то что из него не вылилось ни капли, все чашки наполнились, и кофе потек через край прямо на стол, на платье канониссы.

Она поспешно отставила кофейник, и кофе бесследно исчез.

Оба, Проспер Альпанус и канонисса, молча и несколько странно посмотрели друг на друга.

Глава последняя

Слезная просьба автора.
Как профессор Мош Терпин
успокоился,
а Кандида
уже никогда больше
не могла
рассердиться.
Как золотой жук
прожужжал что-то на ухо
доктору
Просперу Альпанусу
и как тот уехал,
а Бальтазар стал жить
в счастливом
супружестве.

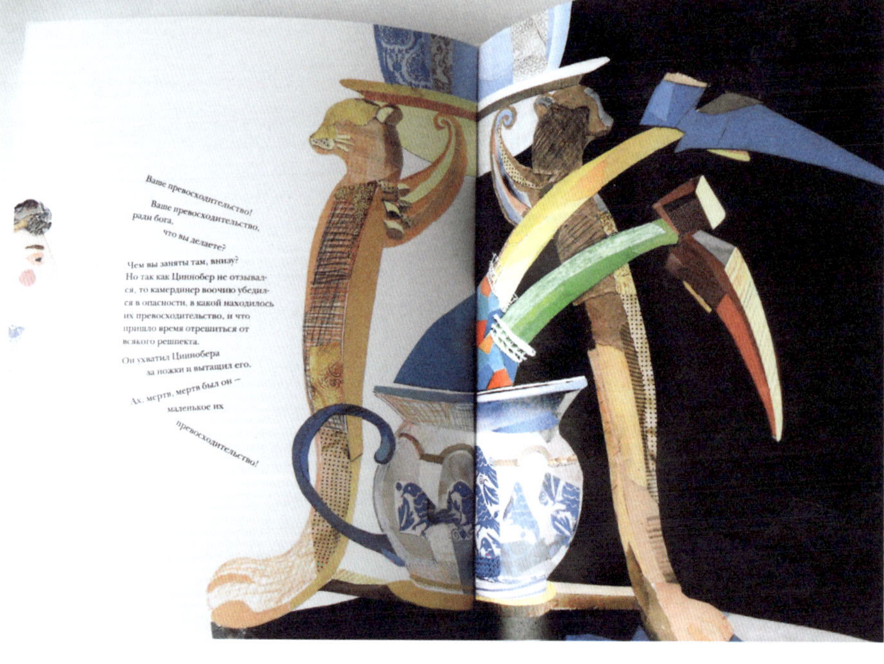

Ваше превосходительство!
Ваше превосходительство,
ради бога,
что вы делаете?

Чем вы заняты там, внизу?
Но так как Циннобер не отзывал-
ся, то камердинер воочию убедил-
ся в опасности, в какой находилось
их превосходительство, и что
пришло время отрешиться от
всякого решпекта.

Он ухватил Циннобера
за ножки и вытащил его.

Ах, мертв, мертв был он —
маленькое их
превосходительство!

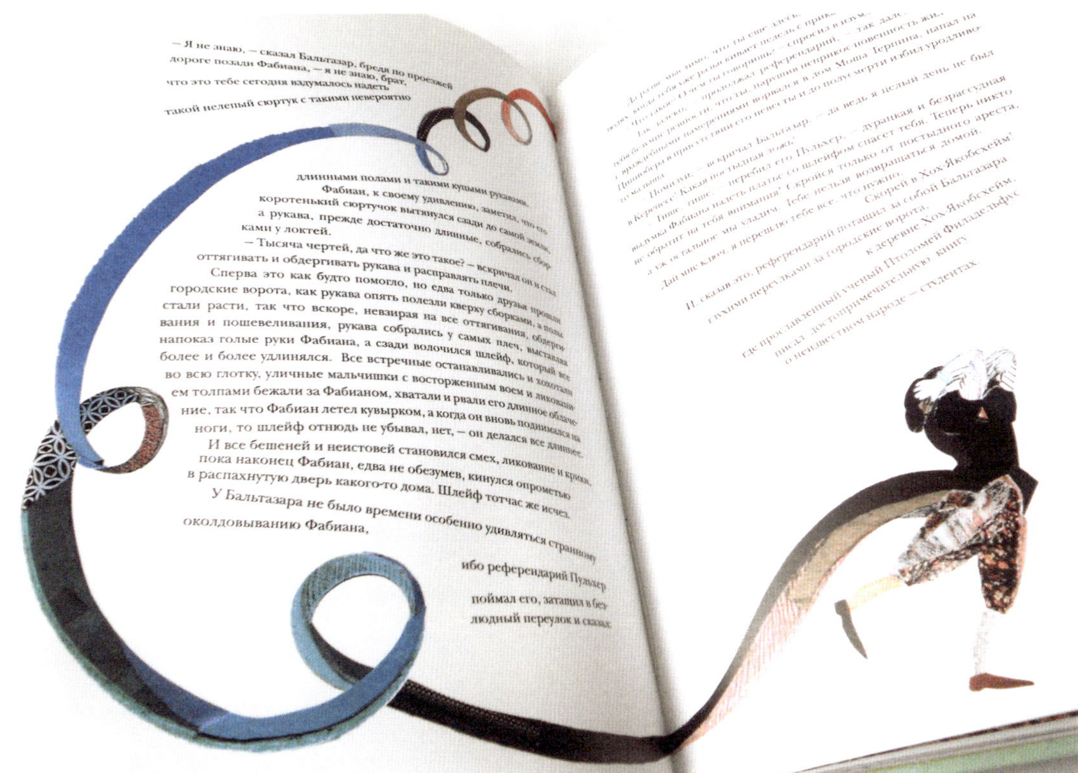

— Я не знаю, — сказал Бальтазар, бредя по проезжей дороге позади Фабиана, — я не знаю, брат, что это тебе сегодня вздумалось надеть такой нелепый сюртук с такими невероятно длинными полами и такими куцыми рукавами.

Фабиан, к своему удивлению, заметил, что его коротенький сюртучок вытянулся сзади до самой земли, а рукава, прежде достаточно длинные, собрались сборками у локтей.

— Тысяча чертей, да что же это такое? — вскричал он и стал оттягивать и обдергивать рукава и расправлять плечи.

Сперва это как будто помогло, но едва только друзья прошли городские ворота, как рукава опять полезли кверху сборками, а полы стали расти, так что вскоре, невзирая на все оттягивания, обдергивания и пошевеливания, рукава собрались у самых плеч, выставляя напоказ голые руки Фабиана, а сзади волочился шлейф, который все более и более удлинялся. Все встречные останавливались и хохотали во всю глотку, уличные мальчишки с восторженным воем и ликованием толпами бежали за Фабианом, хватали и рвали его длинное облачение, так что Фабиан летел кувырком, а когда он вновь поднимался на ноги, то шлейф отнюдь не убывал, нет, — он делался все длиннее.

И все бешеней и неистовей становился смех, ликование и крики, пока наконец Фабиан, едва не обезумев, кинулся опрометью в распахнутую дверь какого-то дома. Шлейф тотчас же исчез.

У Бальтазара не было времени особенно удивляться странному околдовыванию Фабиана,

ибо референдарий Пульхер

поймал его, затащил в безлюдный переулок и сказал:

— Помилуй, — вскричал Бальтазар, — да ведь я целый день не был в Керепесе! Какая постыдная ложь.

— Тише, тише, — перебил его Пульхер, — дурацкая и безрассудная выдумка Фабиана надеть платье со шлейфом спасет тебя. Теперь никто не обратит на тебя внимания! Скройся только от постыдного ареста. Дай мне ключ, я перешлю тебе все, что нужно.

И, сказав это, референдарий потащил за собой Бальтазара глухими переулками за городские ворота. Скорей в Хох-Якобсхейм!

к деревне Хох-Якобсхейм, где прославленный ученый Птоломей Филадельфус писал достопримечательную книгу о неизвестном народе — студентах.

Tales by Borys Grinchenko

Author
Boris Grinchenko

Designer
Oksana Fedko

Size
175mm x 245mm

Completion
2013

Publisher
Master Knyg Printing
Company

'Tales by Borys Grinchenko' contains three stories based on the folklore and ethnographic materials collected by Ukranian author Boris Grinchenko. Oksana Fedko's book is intended to cultivate readers' love and interest in Ukrainian culture, folklore, and folk art. It depicts characters in Ukrainian national dress and explores the nature and symbolism of the fairy tale plot.

Fedko used embroidery—one of the main types of folk art in Ukraine—for the design of this book. The designer took pictures of their grandmother's embroidered pieces, processed the photos in graphic-editing software, and combined embroidered elements with illustrations on a canvas background.

Що царем був у звірів.
Прилітала муха жвава
І казала, що вона
Лева бачила і сили
В світі більшої не зна.
Запеклося коло серця,
Защеміло в комара,
І ніяк забуть не може
Він звірячого царя.
Мучить думка та проклята,
Що від його дужчий є,—

І у серці комаревім
Гордість люта постає.
Ось випростує він крила,
Знявсь і лісом вже летить
Аж туди, де лев могутній,
Пообідавши, лежить.
В сурму голосно ударив:
— Гей ти, леве, уставай!
Будем битися, аж поки
З нас комусь та прийде край.
Бо на цій землі широкій

Зараз побратались;
А як тільки стала нічка,—
З лісу вдвох побрались.
У село приходять тихо,—
Сплять давно вже люди, —
До кошари вдвох підлізли:
— Тут нам здобич буде!
Каже вовк: — Ти все тут знаєш,
Лізь же ти в кошару,
Та відтіль мені і кинеш
Хоч ягняток з пару!

А Сірко ще й радий дуже,—
Вліз він потихеньку
І вовкові викидає
Вже вівцю ситеньку.
Вовк вівцю вхопив і драла,
В гай мерщій тікає;
Наш Сірко з кошари виліз,—
Аж вовка немає!
Озирнувсь Сірко, поглянув
Та із серця й каже:
— Одурив мене вовцюга!

Був колись Сірко-собака,
Жив у чоловіка,
І була йому робота
Дуже невелика:
Од вовків глядіть худобу,
Звіра відганяти,
А удень, як наїсися,
То лягай і спати.
Та Сірко наш був лінивий.
Спав і день, і нічку,

А як спить, вовки і вкрадуть
Гуску чи теличку.
Та Сірко наш не зважає,
Знову ляже спати,—
Злодій прийде та й потягне
Все добро із хати,
Чоловік Сіркові каже:
— Гей, Сірко, не спи ти!
Дурно хліб не можна їсти,
Треба заробити.
На хазяїна розсердивсь

18

19

РИБ'ЯЧІ
ТАНЦІ

Пособляти попросила,
І тоді у них робота
Дуже швидко закипіла:
Кум стромляє ніс у воду,
Рибу з неї викидає,
А лисичка на травиці
Суд над нею вирікає.
І як риба та буває
Повелась негоже в річці,
То злочинницю карати
Доручалося лисичці.
А покараних злочинців

32

Наш Сірко кудлатий:
— Коли так, піду я світа
Кращого шукати!
Ось він з двору вибігає
І біжить до лісу,
Там він зараз зустрічає
Вовчика-гульвісу:
— А, здоров лиш, вовче-брате!
Гризтися нам буде!
Надокучили сердиті

Всі мені ті люди.
Будем ми з тобою жити,
Здобувати їжу
І щодня з тобою будем
Страву мати свіжу:
Знаю я, куди пролізти,
Де живуть ягнята,
Буде наша і теличка,
Гуси й поросята!
Вовк Сіркові радий дуже, —

Кум з кумою не ділили,
А ладненько та тихенько
Так удвох усіх і їли.
І погладшала лисичка,
І така ситенька стала,
Що усіх, як є, довкола
Заздрість звірів обнімала.
Як позаздрили, то стали
Доглядатися пильненько,
Та й дізнались, як лисичка
Порядкує там гарненько.
Пронеслась між звірів чутка

Про її недобре діло,
Слово те й на трон до лева
Трохи згодом долетіло.
Хоч пан лев і сам обіда
Баранами та волами,
А голодний не гидує
І нечистими свинями.
Дак то ж і лев на теє,
Щоб з підданців драти шкуру,
Інш ж мусять мати просту,
А не левову натуру.
Беззаконство він карає:

Сам бажає подивиться,
Як то справді порядкує
Там над рибою лисиця.
Ось до річки він приходе,
А над нею судять саме:
Рибки б'ються на травиці
Головами та хвостами.
Кум з кумою вже гарненько
Пообідати хотіли,
Та зненацька коло себе
Лева дужого уздріли.
— Хто такий ти? Що тут робиш?—

12 Lands

Designers
Yeji Yun, YP

Printing Technology
UV varnish

Size
156mm x 246mm

Completion
2015

Publisher
SSE Project

Yeji Yun often travels the world creating interesting images to record her memories and the journal and picture diary *12 Lands* features illustrations of new landscapes seen by the designer during a year of travel. Yun colors the river orange instead of blue and each star has a different face.

The designer wants children to enjoy each adventure and locate all the journeys on the map at the end of the book. All text is handwritten to feel more personal. This series of illustrations won a YCN Professional Award 2014.

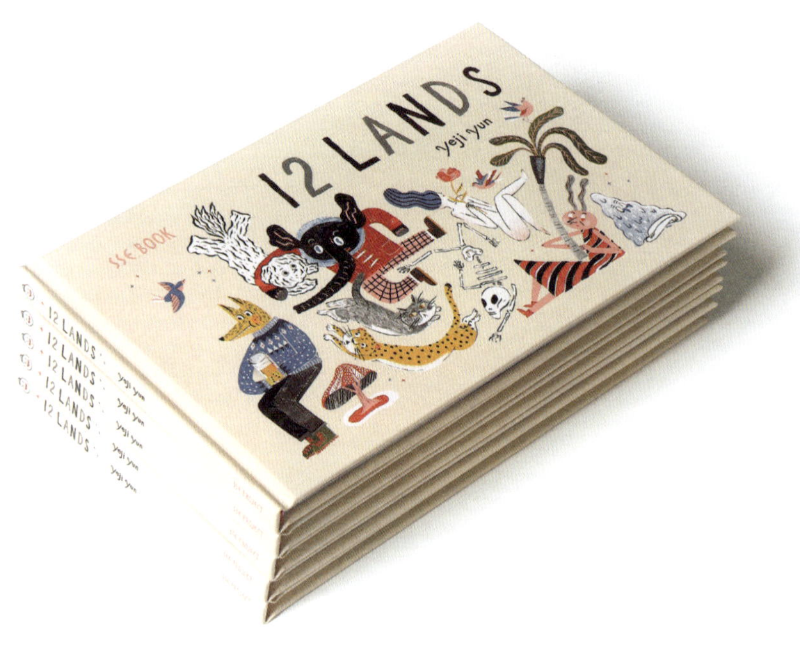

THE NEW ROUND
OF ROAD 365

일 년의 길

ICE SKATING WITH
THE ICE BREAKER

얼음을 깨뜨리는 제창

NIGHT CRUISING
야간 비행

죽음의 땅
DEAD LAND
ICE LAND
얼음땅
FOREST
겨울숲
365 ROUND ROAD 일년의 길
RIVER 강
JUNGLE of HONEY 꿀숲
LAND of FLOOD
범벅이의 땅
FOREST of COIFFURE
미용의 숲
노랑을 모으는 땅
LAND of YELLOW
N
W   E
S
SEA OF CRUISING
비행 바다
BEACH 해변
ISLE of CAT
고양이 섬
12 LANDS

Lady René

Designer
Laura Varsky

Material
118gsm Oxford cream paper

Size
215mm x 215mm

Photo Credit
Laura Varsky

Lady René is a typography catalog created to present designer and illustrator Laura Varsky's lettering work. The narrative is based on the popular late-nineteenth century American song "The Cat Came Back," written by Harry S. Miller, and the book has a final dossier that teaches children what a font is and how fonts are classified. Readers are invited to draw their own fonts at the end of the book.

SE LA ENTREGÓ A UN NIÑO
LE DIO TAMBIÉN UN BILLETE
LE DIJO QUE SE LLEVARA
EN BOTE
Y LA DEJARA AL GARETE
LE AMARRARON UNA CUERDA
AL CUELLO
DEBE HABER PESADO UN KILO
AHORA BUSCAN
EL CUERPO DEL PEQUEÑO
AHOGADO EN EL RÍO

SE LO DIO A UN HOMBRE DE UN GLOBO AEROSTÁTICO
LE PIDIÓ QUE SE LO LLEVARA A UN VIAJE LUNÁTICO
EL GLOBO SE DESINFLÓ A MUCHAS {MUCHAS...} MILLAS
¿QUIÉN SABE DÓNDE ESTÁ?
QUIZÁS EN LAS ANTILLAS.

PERO...
la
GATA

AL DÍA SIGUIENTE
HIZO SU APARECIDA
¡LLEGÓ LA GATA!
NO SOPORTABA ESTAR AUSENTE
MENOS AÚN PERDIDA

EN UN CABLE DE TELÉGRAFO
SE COLUMPIABAN UNOS MIRLOS
LA GATA MUY HAMBRIENTA
HIZO TODO POR COMERLOS

SUBIÓ EL POSTE PASO A PASO
CUIDADOSA, AL ACECHO
PISÓ EL CABLE Y UN NUDO CIEGO
A SU PATA QUEDÓ HECHO

LA GATA ESTABA DE NOVIA
UNA NOCHE EN EL JARDÍN
CANSADOS POR EL RUIDO
LE LANZARON UN BOTÍN
LE DIERON EN LA OREJA,
EL GOLPE
NO PARECÍA GRAVE
PERO LUEGO VOLÓ UN LADRILLO
QUE SE LANZÓ COMO UN AVE.

¡MIAOW!

UNA NOCHE TARDE ANDUVE DE RONDA
SENTÍ TRONAR MUY FUERTE
UNA BOMBA
CON ESTO SÍ QUE TERMINA EL CUENTO
TENDREMOS SEGUROS UN FINAL CRUENTO

PERO...
LA GATA
AL DÍA SIGUIENTE HIZO SU APARECIDA
LLEGÓ LA GATA
{ NO SOPORTABA ESTAR AUSENTE }
MENOS AÚN PERDIDA
IDA... IDA... IDA !
FIN

UNA TIPOGRAFÍA ES UN CONJUNTO DE LETRAS
QUE FORMAN TODO EL ABECEDARIO,
LOS NÚMEROS Y LOS SIGNOS
QUE NECESITAMOS PARA ESCRIBIR
LAS LETRAS
(O CARACTERES)
DE LADY RENÉ
MINÚSCULAS/CAJA BAJA
a b C D E F g H I J K L M
N Ñ O P Q R S T U V W X Y Z
MAYÚSCULAS/CAJA ALTA
A B C D E F G H I J K L M
N Ñ O P Q R S T U V W X Y Z
NÚMEROS Y SIGNOS
0 1 2 3 4 5 6 7 8 9
¿ ? ¡ ! . , . : ; ( ) { } + - % # ®

The Magpie and the Larkspur

Author
Béla Horgas
Designer
René Margit
Illustrator
Anna Láng
Size
185mm x 245mm
Completion
2015

'The Magpie and the Larkspur' (*A Szarka És A Szarkaláb*) is a book of poems by the Hungarian poet and writer Béla Horgas. The poems, illustrated by Anna Láng, are very colorful with plenty of space for imaginative liberties. Many of Horgas's poems are about nature, such as flowers, wind, and clouds, and the plant illustrations have a botanic feel to enrich the educational function of the book. Interesting, faded textures and mixed colors are kept in harmony.

Margit makes all the publications for Liget Mūhely Publishing House and the typography always follows the same format with a playful font for titles and a very simple and clear font for texts.

SZAMÁR-DALOK

Fönn a létrán ül egy szamár,
háta porzik, így ordibál,
esőt szomjaz, lóg a füle,
szebben szól a fülemüle!
Hej, te müle, te szamár,
ma is már és holnap is,
szamár leszek magam is,
már ma szamár, szama-már!

Fönn a létrán konya füllel
ül egy szamár, és mit művel?
Orrán drótos okuláré,
néz, de nem lát – boldog málé!
Hej, te málé, te szamár,
széna-szalma, jobb és bal,
némaságnál jobb a dal,
már ma szamár, szama-már!

Fönn a létrán: szürke, szürke,
ül egy szamár elmerülve,
ábrándjába berámázva,
mit neki a süket lárma!
Ó, az ábránd, te szamár,
csökött álom, deres kóró,
testre szabott, névre szóló,
szürke szamár, szama-már!

SZAMÁRLÉTRA

Kánya bánja,
vigye ördög,
szerdára meg-
jön csütörtök.

péntek, szombat
és vasárnap –
de jó, de jó
a szamárnak!

Egész héten
csak iázik,
hétfőn, kedden
csacsit játszik.

szerdán szalad,
jön csütörtök,
kánya bánja,
vigye ördög,

péntekre meg-
jön a szombat,
szombaton a
szamárszombat

szamárlétrát
nyújt a hétnek,
szamarai
heherésznek:

gyehe-rehe,
jöjj, vasárnap!
De jó, de jó
a szamárnak!

LAKODALMI SZERENÁD – VIRÁGOK NEVÉRE

Csilláros sárma, nyúlszapuka!
Leszek még nálad:
megyek még hozzád:
erdei lórom, szürke müge.
Szürke müge.

Varádics, kákics, halvány aszat!
Eljössz majd hozzám,
itt maradsz nálam:
gurgolya, perje, csomós ebír!
Csomós ebír!

Cickafark, zászpa, szamárkenyér!
Itt vagyok érted,
szeretlek téged:
mácsonya, kosbor, fehér üröm!
Fehér üröm...

Tarsóka, gémorr, nagy bakszakáll!
Menyegző nyílik,
éjszaka múlik –
jajrózsa, tömjén, szalmagyopár.
Szalmagyopár.

Gyilkhagyma, szümcső, macskagyökér!
Két virág egy pár:
zsombor és hölgymál,
zsurló és tippan – bábakalács!
Bábakalács.

AZ ÉN CIRKUSZOM

Nem veszélyes,
egyszemélyes,
mindig nagyon leleményes
az én cirkuszom!
Van benne majom!
Mászik a falon.
Van benne zsiráf!
Félti a nyakát.
Van benne minden:
mesés a kincsem –
ha elképzelem...

Nem veszélyes,
egyszemélyes,
mindig nagyon leleményes
az én cirkuszom...
Van benne, tudom,
árnyék a falon,
van benne teve,
gyémánt a feje,
van benne tündér –
hozzám jöhetnél!

UBORKA-DAL

Petrezselyem petrencében,
bolond világ félfektében,
Kapor Klára sír magában,
ott lakik egy uborkában.
Hét törpe jő, mind-mind bátor,
egyikük sincs puha fából.
Mese mátka, gyöngyök, álom,
átlibbenünk hét határon,
selyemfűből lágy petrence,
hogyan tehetnék kedvedre?
Mintha gonosz nem is volna –
most szólalj meg, zöld uborka!

KAPTAFA

Volt egyszer egy kaptafa,
tornyában a fakapta.

Ki kaptafát nem látott,
nem látta a világot.

kapta fája, kaptafa,
világ végén áll a fa.

fából van a kaptafa,
kaptából a fakapta.

világ fája, kaptája,
ugorjunk a tornyába.

*

Kaptafa lába,
cipő a háza,

kaptafa ága,
ne állj alája.

kaptafa álma,
gubbaszt magába.

lába és álma,
háza és ága

mindig magába –
ne állj alája.

*

Kaptafából van a kaptár,
magtafából meg a magtár.

de a naptár miből van?
Naptafából van talán?

Kapta, magta, naptafácska,
kerek erdő három fája.

miből van hát a naptár?
Naptafából van talán?

*

Egy magányos kaptafa
ökrét, házát eladta,

szívét bánat vette meg,
bánatában megrepedt.

Repedt szívvel mit tehet?
Keservesen füttyöget.

TAVASZI
TÖRTÉNET

Szervusz, mókusz, szólt a krókusz,
tavasz van már? Te mit gondolsz?
Ugyan, krókus, így a mókus,
minek ez a hókus-pókus?
Mit kérdezel? Nem hírt hoztál?
Talán meg is náthásodtál,
vagy pösze vagy, pici krókus,
mondd utánam szépen: mókus.
Pösze, te meg pisze, mókusz,
vágott vissza a kis krókusz.

Napestig így viccelődtek,
zöldült a hegy, rügyek nőttek,
a mókus bukfencet vetett,
a krókusz azt mondta, remek,
és barátok lettek, tényleg.
Tavasszal ez megtörténhet.

RÍMKEVERŐ

Nem afféle
rusnyaféle
vásári
szájtáti,
nem amolyan
utcasarki
semmire se kellő
félnótás tekergő –
de maga a költő,
a talányos,
zöld köpenyes
mutatványos,
kék nadrágos
csodatevő,
maga a nagy
rímkeverő
került
a semmiből elő –
térült-fordult,
kevert-kavart,
sose láttam
ilyen vihart:
hetet-havat
összehordott,
ujja hegyén
világ forgott,
külön világ –
külön ajtó,
külön ablak...
Szólt a költő:
Hamm! Bekaplak!

PAPÍRJÁTÉK

Egy ír pap
és egy skót tapir
egymásnak levelet ír
egy parányi pirosra
egy kitépett, árva papirosra,
ám mert az ír pap
nem tud tapirul, sem skótul
és a skót tapir sem
írul vagy papul –
levelet egymásnak
hiába ír
a pap és a tapir.

Megmondom neked, boszorkány,
nyakadba csördít hat orkán.

Megmondom neked, rád rivall,
hajad kitépi hét vihar.

Megmondom neked, ne számolj,
tenyeres-talpas – ficánkol.

Megmondom neked, elég volt:
szél a szelekkel eliszkolt.

*

Sötétben is fúj a szél,
hosszú lába földig ér,
szél, szél, szél.

Eresz alján kopogtat.
Ne hajolj ki, megfoghat,
szél, szél szél.

*

Szél vesszeje,
ereje,
torka –
kilukadt terem,
ordító csatorna.
Szél sörénye,
lába –
zablavasak,
fogak csikorgása.
Leszakadt ajtó.
Völgyekből fölkapott
harangos harangszó.
Szél.
Vesszeje, ereje, torka.
Éjszaka
arcom bekormozza.

Charlie and the Chocolate Factory

Author
Roald Dahl

Designer
Ane Erkomaishvili

Material
180gsm coated gloss paper

Size
250mm x 210mm

Completion
2013

Charlie and the Chocolate Factory is a world-renowned story. Due to the many adaptations of the book, this project required the creation of a new visual representation, which proved reasonably challenging for the designer. Ane Erkomaishvili mixed pencil and digital techniques to create an original style that would bring the story alive once again.

The mysterious and eccentric chocolatier Willy Wonka is one of the most important visual aspects of the project. However, unlike previous adaptations, the image of Willy Wonka is not fully defined in this version. Instead, he is represented mostly as a silhouette, leaving room for the reader's imagination to define the character and encouraging a deeper level of engagement with the story.

The book contains some removable extras that enable children to interact further with the book. These include two envelopes, with the golden ticket and the newspaper featuring Willy Wonka's notice, and a television set with Mike Teavee on screen.

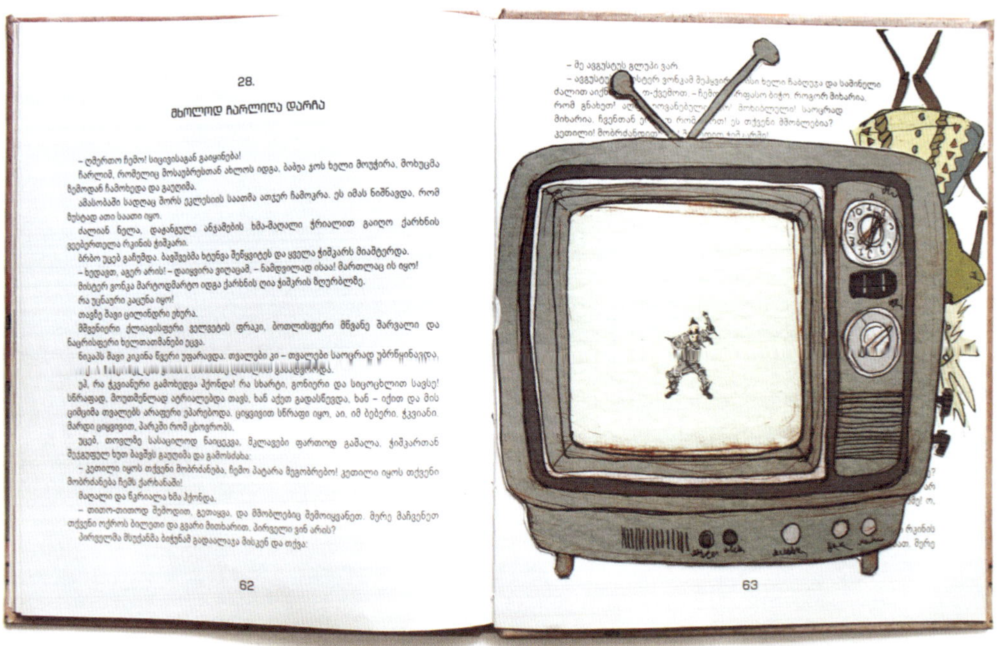

– ჭკვიანი?! – შეჰყვირა მოხუცმა, – ჭკვიანი კი არა, გენიოსია! შოკოლადის ჯადოქარია! რა გინდა, რომ არ გააკეთოს! განა მართალს არ გამბობ, ჩემო ძვირფასებო?

მოხუცებმა ზანტად დააკანტურეს თავები, სრულ ჯემშარიტებას ამბობო.

– ნუთუ არასოდეს მიამშნია მენთვის მისტერ ვილი ვონკასა და მის ქარხანაზე?

– არასოდეს, – თავი გააქნია პატარა ჩარლიმ.

– ღმერთო დიდებულო! ეს როგორ დამე-მართა?!

– ახლა მიამბე, რა, ბაბუა ჯო.

– რა თქმა უნდა, გიამბობ. საღოლზე ჩამომიჯექი, ჩემო ძვირფასო, და კარგად დამიგდე ყური.

ბაბუა ჯომ 96 წელს გადააბიჯა, ჩარლის ბაბუებსა და ბებიებს შორის ყველაზე ხნიერი და ამიტომაც ყველაზე სუსტი და უძლური გახლდათ. ერთ-ორ სიტყვას თუ ამოიღუღლუღებდა ხოლმე მთელი დღის განმავლობაში. საღამოობით კი, როცა მისი საყვარელი შვილიშვილი ჩარლი ენგელდათ, სასნაულებრივად ახალგაზრდავდებოდა, ჯან-ღონე ემატებოდა და ჭაბუკივით ენერგიული ხდებოდა.

– ოჰ, რომ იცოდე, ვინ არის ეს მისტერ ვილი ვონკა! – შეჰყვირა ბაბუა ჯომ, – პირადად მან გამოიგონა შოკოლადის ორასზე მეტი ახალი სახეობა, ერთმანეთისგან სრულიად ფილები დახსენით-მეთქი! ასეც მოიქცნენ. დილიდან საღამომდე იჯდა ყველა მუშა ქალი და შოკოლადის ფილებს ხსნიდა.

მაგრამ სამი დღე ისე გავიდა, ბედმა არ გაგვიღიმა. ოჰ, რა სამშინელება იყო! ჩემი პატარა ვერუკა დღითიდღე უფრო მფოთავდა და შინ დაბრუნებულს შემომკივლებდა ხოლმე, სად არის ჩემი ოქროს ბილეთი, ჩემი ოქროს ბილეთი მინდაო; განწვებოდა იატაკზე, ტლინკებს აყრიდა და გულისწამღებად კიოდა. გული მიკვდებოდა, ჩემს პატარას ასეთ უბედურს რომ ვხედავდი, ჰოდა, დავიფიცე, მანამ განვაგრძობდი ძებნას, სანამ არ ვიპოვიდი ვერუკას სანუკვარ ბილეთს. უცბად...

მეოთხე საღამოს, ერთ-ერთმა ქალმა

ორი ოეროს ბილეთი კიდევ იპოვეს

– აპ-აპ... ეს კი... ეს მისტერ ვონკას კიდევ ერთი ჭკვიანური გამოგონებაა.

– ჩარლი, ძვირფასო, – დაუქახა მისის ბაკეტმა, – ძილის დროა. დანარჩენი ამბავი სხვა დროს იყოს.

– მაგრამ, დედა, ძალიან მაინტერესებს...

– ხვალ, ჩემო ძვირფასო...

– მართალია, – უთხრა ბაბუა ჯომ, – დანარჩენს ხვალ გიამბობ.

მეორე საღამოს ბაბუა ჯომ ისევ განაგრძო თხრობა.

მეორე საღამოს ბაბუა ჯომ ისევ განაგრძო თხრობა.

– არცთუ დიდი ხნის წინათ მისტერ ვონკას ქარხანაში ათასობით ადამიანი მუშაობდა. მერე ეგრად ვონკა იძულებული გახდა, სათითაოდ დაეთხოვა ყველა.

– რატომ? – იკითხა ჩარლიმ.

– ჯაშუშების გამო.

– ჯაშუშების?

– დიახ. სხვა შოკოლადის მკეთებლებს შეშურდათ მისტერ ვონკასი და ჯაშუშები მიუჩინეს მისი საიდუმლო რეცეპტების მოსაპარად. ჯაშუშები ჩვეულებრივი მუშებივით იწყებდნენ მისტერ ვონკას ქარხანაში მუშაობას და იქ ყოფნისას სწავლობდნენ, როგორ კეთდებოდა ესა თუ ის ნუგბარი.

– მერე ბრუნდებოდნენ თავიანთ ქარხნებში და ვონკას საიდუმლოს გასცემდნენ? – იკითხა ჩარლიმ.

– ალბათ, – უპასუხა ბაბუა ჯომ, – რადგან მერე ფიკელგრუბერის ქარხანამ ისეთი ნაყინის გამოშვება დაიწყო, რომელსაც ყველაზე მცხუნვარე მზეც კი ვერ ადნობდა; მისტერ პროდნოუსის ქარხანამ

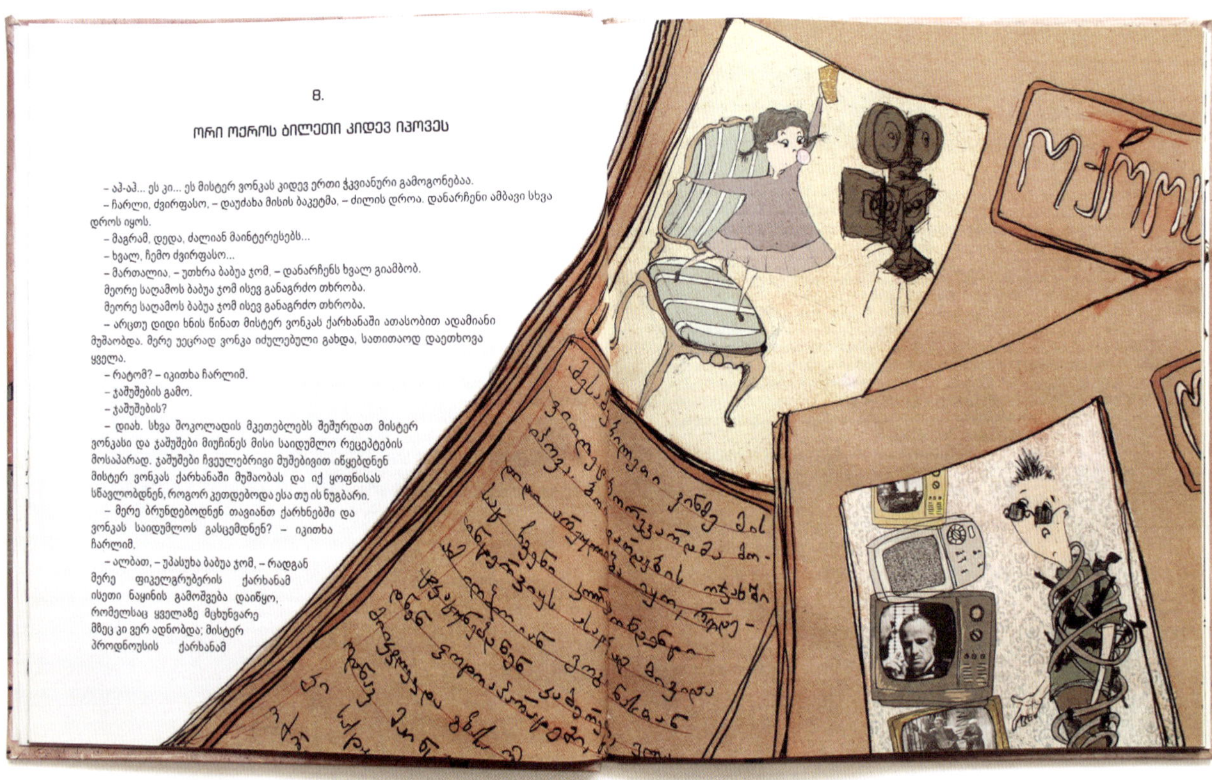

ისეთი სალექი რეზინის კეთება დაიწყო, რამდენიც უნდა გელეჭა, გემო არ ეკარგებოდა. მისტერ სლაგვორთის ქარხანამ დაამზადა შაქრის ტკბილი ბურთულები, რომლებიც უსაშველოდ იბერებოდა და შექმამდე ქინძისთავით უნდა გაგეხეთქა. ერთი სიტყვით, ისე ნავიდა საქმე, მისტერ ვილი ვონკა წვერს იგლეჯდა და ყვიროდა:

– ეს რა სამინელებაა! ასე ხომ გავკოტრდები! ირგვლივ ჯაშუშები მახვევია! ნამდვილად ქარხნის დახურვა მომიწევს!

– ჰო, მაგრამ, რომ არ დაუხურავს?! – იკითხა ჩარლიმ.

– დახურა. ყველა მუშა დაითხოვა, მთავარი შესასვლელი ჩარაზა და ჯაჭვით ჩაკეტა! შედეგად, ვონკას ვეებერთელა შოკოლადის ქარხანა მიყუჩდა, იქაურობა გამოყრუვდა, საკვამურებიდან ბოლი აღარ ამოდიოდა, მანქანები აღარ გეგუნებდა და მას მერე შოკოლადი ან რაიმე ტკბილეული აღარ გაკეთებულა. კაციშვილი არ შესულა, არც გამოსულა იქიდან და მისტერ ვილი ვონკაც გაუჩინარდა... თვე თვეს მისდევდა, – განაგრძობდა ბაბუა ჯო, – მაგრამ ქარხანა მაინც დაკეტილი იყო. ყველა ამბობდა, საწყალი მისტერ ვონკა, რა კარგი კაცი იყო და რა საოცარ რამეებს აკეთებდა, მორჩა მისი ამბავი.

გავიდა ხანი და განსაცვიფრებელი რამ მოხდა: ერთ დღეს, დილაადრიან, მოქალაქეებმა დაინახეს, რომ ვონკას საკვამურებიდან თეთრი ბოლი ამოდიოდა! ხალხი ჩერდებოდა და მისჩერებოდა.

– ნეტავ რა ხდება? – ყვიროდნენ ისინი, – ვიდაცას ღუმელი დაუნთია, ალბათ მისტერ ვონკა ისევ ხსნის თავის ქარხანას! – ყველანი ჯიშკარს მისცვივდნენ, ეგონათ, დაინახავდნენ, როგორ ეგებებოდა მისტერ ვონკა თავის მუშებს.

მაგრამ ნურას უკაცრავად! უზარმაზარი რკინის ჯიშკარი გულდაგულ იყო ჩარაზული და მისტერ ვონკაც არსად ჩანდა.

– აბა, ქარხანა რომ მუშაობს! – ყვიროდა ხალხი, – ხომ გესმით მანქანების გუგუნი! პაერშიც შოკოლადის სუნი ტრიალებს!

ბაბუა ჯო წინ გადაიხარა, გრძელი, დამჭკნარი თითი ჩარლის მუხლზე დააღო და ჩურად უთხრა:

– სასწაული კი ის იყო, ჩარლი, რომ ქარხნის ფანჯრებში ჩრდილები ჩანდა, გარეთ მიდგა, როგორ მოძრაობდნენ მაცალა, ყუჩი ჩრდილები მიმის

– ვისი ჩრდილები? – სწრაფად იკითხა ჩარლიმ.

– ამის გაგება ყველას აინტერესებს.

– შენობა მუშებითაა სავსე! – ყვიროდა ხალხი, – შიგ რომ არავინ შესულა! ჯიშკარიც ჩაკეტილია! გასაგიჟებელია პირდაპირ! არც არავინ გამოდის იქიდან!

– მაგრამ ექვიც არ იყო, რომ ქარხანა მუშაობდა, – განაგრძობდა ბაბუა ჯო, – მას მერე ათი წელია, სულ მუშაობს. უფრო მეტიც, თანდათან უფრო და უფრო საოცარი და გემრიელი

შოკოლადები და ტკბილეული მზადდება. და ახლა, რალა თქმა უნდა, მისტერ ვონკას გამოგონილ ახალ, მშვენიერ ტკბილეულს ვერც მისტერ ფიკელგრებერი გადაიღებს, ვერც მისტერ პროდნოუსი და ვერც მისტერ სლაგვორთი ან სხვა ვინმე. ვერავითარი ჯაშუში ვეღარ შეაღწევს ვილი ვონკას ქარხანაში.

– კი მაგრამ, ბაბე, – შეჰკვირა ჩარლიმ, – ვის ამუშავებს მისტერ ვონკა თავის ქარხანაში?

– არავინ იცის.

– რა სისულელეა! განა არავის ეკითხავს მისტერ ვონკასთვის?

– არავის უნახავს მისტერ ვონკა, რადგან გარეთ არასოდეს გამოსულა. იქიდან შოკოლადებისა და ტკბილეულის გარდა გარეთ არავინ და არაფერი გამოდის. ტკბილეულს კი. უკვე შეფუთულს და მისამართდაწერილს, საგანგებო გვირაბით ყოველდღე ეზიდებიან საფოსტო მანქანები.

– ბაბუ, ნეტა რა ხალხი მუშაობს იქ?

– ჩემო ძვირფასო ბიჯუნა, – უთხრა ბაბუა ჯომ, – ეს შოკოლადმკეთებელი სამყაროს უდიდესი საიდუმლოებაა. მათ შესახებ მხოლოდ ის ვიცით, რომ კუკები არიან. ის ერთი ციცქნა მქრქალი ჩრდილები ზოგჯერ, განსაკუთრებით გვიან ღამით, შექზე რომ მოჩანან ფანჯრის მიდმა, მუხლამდე თუ მომწვდებიან...

და მისტერ ბაკეტმა რომ საღამოს გაზეთი მოიტანა, პირველ გვერდზე მისი დიდი სურათი დაებეჭდათ. ავგუსტუსი ცხრა წლის ეზომოდ ჩასუქებული ბიჭი იყო, გეგონებოდათ, ტუმბოთი გაუბერიათო. ტანზე ქონები ეკიდა, სახე უზარმაზარ ცომის გუნდას მიეგავდა. წვრილი, ხარბი თვალებით შეჰყურებდა ქვეყნიერებას. გაზეთში ეწერა, თერმე ქალაქი, სადაც ავგუსტუს გლუპი ცხოვრობს, ადფრთოვანებისაგან ლამის შეიშალა, ბილეთი რომ მათ გმირს შეხვდა. ფანჯრებზე დროშები გამოკიდეს, ბავშვები სკოლიდან დაითხოვეს და ამ სახელგანთქმული ბიჭუნას პატივსაცემად ალღემი მოაწყვეს.

ბავშვები ჩაქუჩებით ამსხვრევდნენ თავიანთ ყელაბებს და ფელი
მუჯედატენილები გარბოდნენ მადა-ზიებისკენ ერთ ქალაქში ვიდა
ცნობილმა ბანდიტმა ბანკიდან ათასი ფენტი გაიტაცა და შეადლუე
მთლიანად ვონკას შოკოლადების ფილეებში დახარჯა. ხოლო რ ჟა
პოლიციადასაპა-ტიმრებლადმიხმიადგა. ნახეს, რომიატაკზედახვ
შოკოლადებში მოერთხა ფეხი და ქალალდებს. რომლებშიც მ
იყო მეფუთელი. გრძელი სატევრის პირით ხსნიდა. შორეულ რ
მცხოვრები ქალი. მარლოტ რუსი, ამტკიცებდა. მეორე ბილეთი ვ
მაგრამ თურმე თალითითობდა. ცნობილმა ინგლისელმა სნავ
პროფესორმა ფოულბოდიმ გამოიგონა მანქანა. რომელიც
ფილის გაუხსნელად გამოიცნობდა. იყო თუ არა შიგ ოქროს
მანქანას მექანიკური თათი ჰქონდა. საოცარი ძალით გამოვარ
და ჩაბლუკავდა. სადმე ოქროს ნასახიც რომ ეპოვა მიმალუე
უკვეთესი თითქოს რაია უნდა გამოევგონებინათ. მაგრამ, საებე
როცა პროფესორი თავის მანქანას უზარმაზარ მალაზიაში ტკბილე
დახლთან საზოგადოებას აჩვენებდა. მექანიკური თათი გამო
იქვე მდგომ პერცოვინიას ოქროს პროთუკბის ბოლო კბილს ჩაა
ამაზე ერთი ამბავი შეიქნა და გაშმაგებულ ბრბოს მანქანა შემოე

ჩარლი ბაკეტის იებილეედდ ერთი დლით ადრე გაზე
გამოაცხადეს, მეორე ოქროს ბილეთიც იპოვესო. ეს ბედნიერე
პატარა გოგოს – ვერუკა სოლტს ხვდა. იგი სადაც შორს, დიდ
ცხოვრობდა მდიდარ მშობლებთან ერთად. მისტერ ბაკეტმა
გაზეთი რომ მოიტანა. ისევ დაებეჯდათ მპოვნელის დიდი ს
საკუთარი სახლის სასტუმრო ოთახში იჯდა სახეგაბადრულ მშ
შორის, ოქროს ბილეთს მალლა იჭნევდა და იკრიჭებოდა.

მისტერ სოლტმა, ვერუკას მამამ, მგზ-ნებარედ
ჟურნალისტებს, როგორ იპოვეს ბილეთი. ˌიგი
ახალგაზრდებო. როგორც კი ჩემმა პატარა გოგონამ
ერთ-ერთი ოქროს ბილეთი მეც უნდა მქონდესო,
ნავედი და რამდენიც შევძელი, ვონკას შოკოლადი
ფილა ვიყიდე. ათასობით მაინც მაქვს ნაყიდი, ის კი არ
ათასობითაც! მერე სატვირთო მანქანები დავატვირ
პირდაპირ ჩემს ქარხანაში გავგზავნე. მე მინისთხილზე
ასამდე მუშა ქალი მყავს დაქირავებული. ისინი თხილ
აცლიან და მოსახალად ამზადებენ. დილიდან სადამდ

History of
Black Stone

Designer
Katarzyna Breczko

Size
210mm x 280mm

Completion
2012

The main character and narrator in 'History of Black Stone' (*Historia Czarnego Kamienia*) is a lump of coal named Carbon. The book introduces readers to the world of mining and discusses its role in the history of civilization. The story is intended to help children understand the importance of the work of their great grandparents and black-and-white illustrations are drawn with pencil and charcoal to express the topic of the book.

W labiryncie podziemnych korytarzy na górników czyhało bardzo dużo niebezpieczeństw. Panowała tam wysoka temperatura, było duszno, a w powietrzu unosiły się bardzo groźne gazy – dwutlenek węgla przy podłodze oraz pył węglowy i metan. Niebezpieczne substancje w każdej chwili mogły wybuchnąć, kiedy było ich za dużo w powietrzu. Najgorsze jest to, że gazy te są niewidzialne i pozbawione zapachu. Nie dało się przewidzieć, kiedy zagrożenie życia jest blisko. Górnicy odkryli, że istnieją mali przyjaciele, którzy o wiele wcześniej wyczuwają niebezpieczeństwo. Zabierali ze sobą samiczki kanarków, które bardzo lubią śpiewać. Kiedy milknęły, siedziały osowiałe, a górnik wiedział, że trzeba się stamtąd jak najszybciej ewakuować. Niejeden taki ptaszek uratował im życie, poświęcając swoje własne. W kopalni można było spotkać także szczury. Kiedy zbliżało się niebezpieczeństwo, to niewielkie zwierzątko wiedziało o tym o wiele wcześniej i biegło w bezpieczne miejsce. Uciekające szczury – były także znakiem dla górnika, że za niedługo stanie się coś złego!

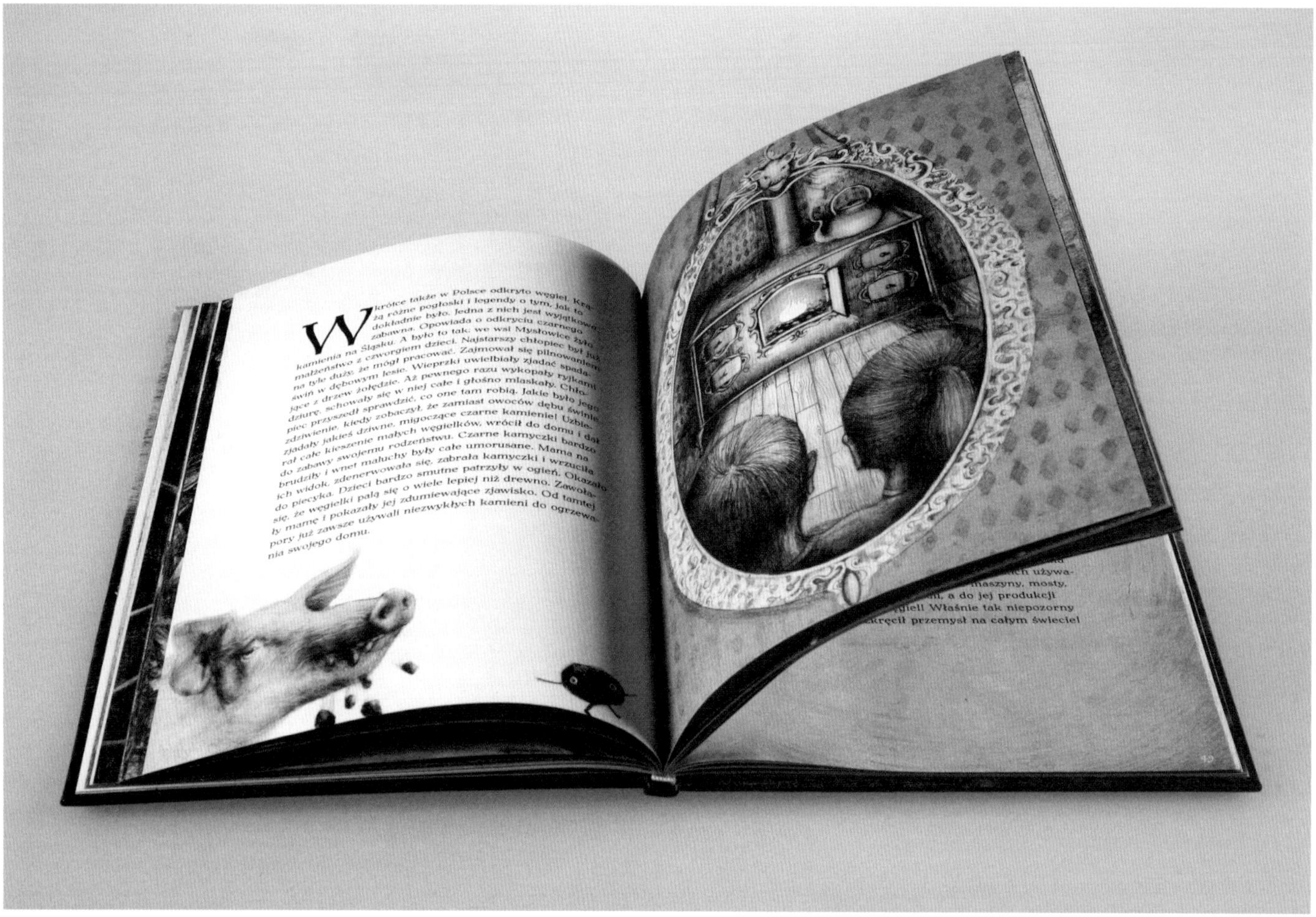

CZAPKA
KAMIZELKA
KOSZULA
SKÓRZANA ŁATA
WYSOKIE BUTY
MŁOT
ŻELAZKO
KARBITKA
CZARNY PROCH

Wszystko zaczęło się w XVIII wieku w Anglii. Było to wtedy najbogatsze i najbardziej zaludnione państwo świata. Ludzie żyli coraz dłużej. Było ich też coraz więcej, więc potrzeba było coraz więcej materiałów, aby ich wszystkich ubrać. Aby uszyć ubrania potrzeba było coraz więcej tkanin. Tkaniny produkowano ręcznie w wielkich manufakturach. Zamówień było coraz więcej i więcej. Nawet tysiące rąk nie nadążało. W 1733 roku pewien sukiennik, John Kay wymyślił maszynę do tkania materiałów, którą nazwał „Latające czółenko mechaniczne", tkacze dzięki niej mogli pracować dwa razy szybciej. Tak lawina wielkich wynalazków została uruchomiona. Producenci maszyn potrzebowali coraz więcej stali, szli do właścicieli hut, właściciele hut potrzebowali coraz więcej drewna, aby wytopić stal. Wycinano ogromne połacie lasów, aż w końcu władca Anglii wydał zakaz karczowania, obawiając się że wkrótce w jego kraju nie będzie już drzew. Przemysł na chwilę zwolnił. Szukano nowego paliwa.

Prawie sto lat od tego wielkiego odkrycia świat ogarnęła druga, ogromna rewolucja przemysłowa. Naukowcy wymyślili coś jeszcze lepszego niż para wodna! Prąd elektryczny! W 1831 roku skonstruowano pierwsze urządzenie, którym można było przesyłać informacje na odległość. Kilkadziesiąt lat później Thomas Edison udoskonalił żarówkę elektryczną, a dwa lata później zbudował pierwszą elektrownię – miejsce, w którym wytwarzany jest prąd i potem przesyłany wielką siecią kabli do wszystkich domów. Prądu elektrycznego można było używać nie tylko do oświetlania, ale także do napędzania maszyn. Przez długie lata powoli maszyny parowe były zastępowane przez elektryczne. Te pierwsze bardzo rzadko są dziś używane, mimo, że były one bardzo trwałe i wiele z nich mogłoby nadal pracować. To wszystko nie znaczy, że węgiel stał się niepotrzebny. Nadal był i wciąż jest potrzebny do produkcji stali i wielu innych rzeczy, bez których przemysł nie mógłby się rozwijać. Oprócz elektrowni węglowych istnieje także wiele elektrowni wodnych, jądrowych, słonecznych. Podziemia kopalni również bardzo się zmieniały, ponieważ trzeba było coraz szybciej wydobywać węgiel. Pojawiły się pierwsze kolejki elektryczne oraz mnóstwo innych urządzeń, przyspieszających pracę górników. Nie zmieniło się tylko jedno. Górnik nadal jest potrzebny pod ziemią. Teraz zamiast żelazka i młotu obsługuje wielkie maszyny.

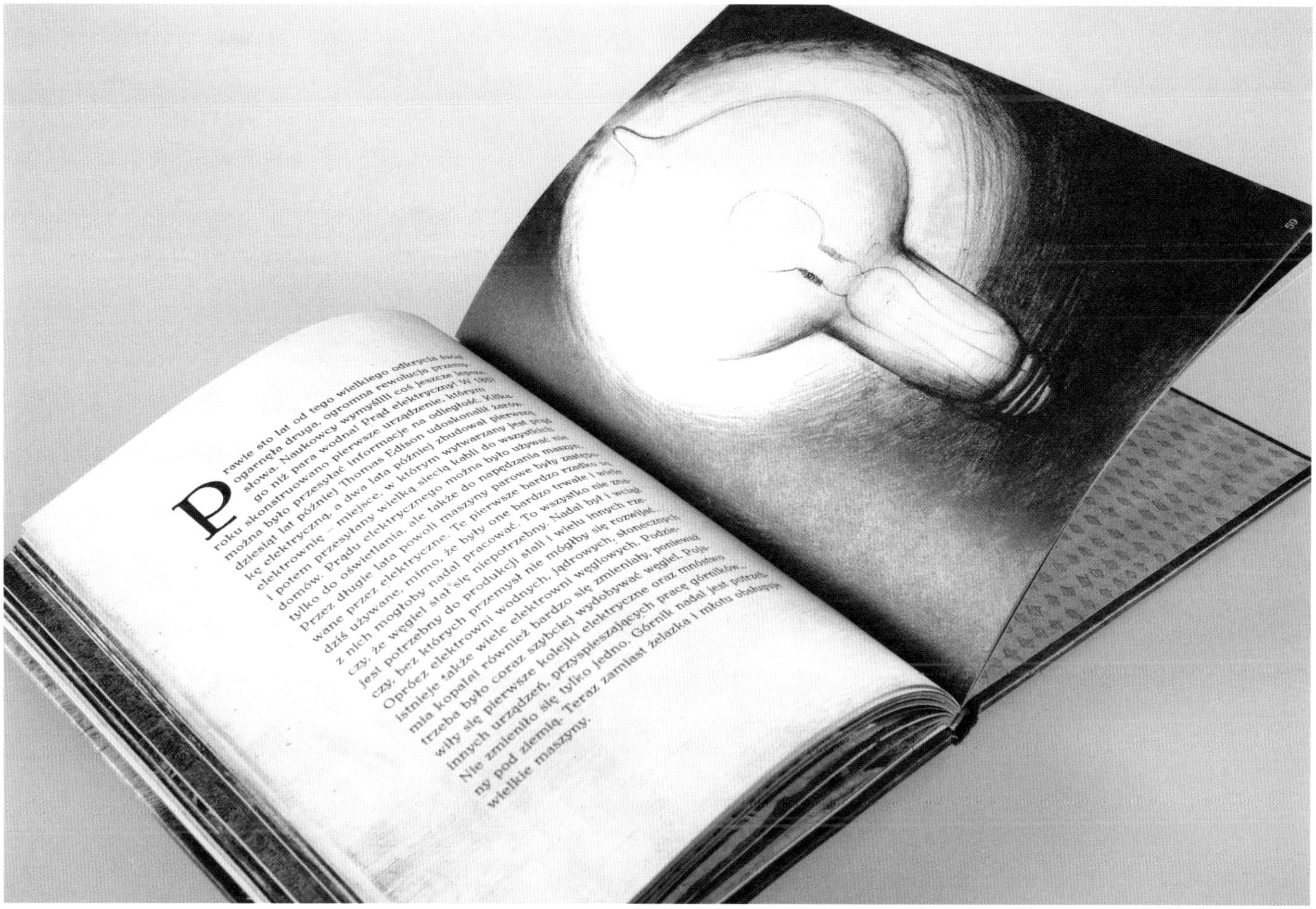

The History
of a Star

Author
Anna Kazeykina
Designer
Ekaterina Kazeykina
Size
207mm x 275mm
Completion
2013

Two sisters created 'The History of a Star.' Anna Kazeykina wrote an allegorical parable about human values and star manufacturing while Ekaterina Kazeykina helped compose the text and designed the book. The form of the book and the genre of the story is suitable for both children and adults.

The illustrations echo different narrative levels of the story by combining blank surfaces with pictures that have depth and perspective. Each spread presents a metaphorical character in historic costume in a contemporary situation. While the text is brief, the content emphasizes the symbolic aspect of the story. The final spread invites readers to interact with the book with a third leaf that unfolds to reveal a fully illustrated three-page panorama without text. Thus, the final outcome of the story is expressed in pictures.

"

В понедельник утром первая городская
Модница попросила россыпь звезд для нового
платья. Приближался бал у губернатора.
Созвездие назвали в честь царицы
Кассиопеи, которая хвалилась, будто
она красивее всех на свете.

Последним прибежал городской чиновник
и заказал большую звезду, чтобы светила ярче,
чем фонарь на главной площади.

Once Upon an Alphabet

Designer
Oliver Jeffers

Printing Technology
Matte foil stamping

Size
235mm x 320mm

Completion
2014

Publisher
**HarperCollins UK,
Philomel Books US.**

Oliver Jeffers's story is a unique and playful ode to the 26 letters of the alphabet. *Once Upon an Alphabet* strings together a series of paradoxes, perplexities, and unintended consequences with witty, lyrical, and charmingly irreverent design.

Subtle connections and clever asides are hidden throughout and bright colors let the reader know this is not a classic alphabet book. The heavy paper stock, spot color treatment, and typeface are inspired by Jeffers's own childhood picture books.

A B C D E F G
H I J K L M
N O P Q R S T
U V W X Y Z

Xx

One terrible morning, Xavier woke to discover that his excellent pair of x-ray spectacles had been stolen.

He knew exactly who to call…

What the owl and the octopus knew, that the burglar did not, was that an extra pair existed.

Y

Mr. Badger's Rhymes

Designers
Romana Ruban,
Antony Slatvinskiy

Material
300gsm and 150gsm
Munken Lynx paper

Size
110mm x 160mm

Completion
2015

'Mr. Badger's Rhymes' is a book in which the designers imagine badgers and other animals as people of different professions and natures. The designers drew childlike characters with shaded pencil in gray, black, and white, hoping their approach would encourage young readers to bring their fantasies and ideas to life.

The designers used Munken Lynx paper for its shade and texture. Unique and creative features are intended to make reading more attractive and interactive. Cut-out windows and folded pages allow readers to see the characters through the pages.

ДІВЧИНКА БОРСУКА ПІЙМАЛА — ПРИГОСТИЛА ЙОГО КАКАО. КОЖЕН ВЕЧІР БІЛЯ ВІКОНЦЯ ЧЕКАЄ ТА ПІСЕНЬКИ ПРО НЬОГО СКЛАДАЄ.
БОРСУК ТАКИЙ ВЕСЕЛИЙ ТА ХОРОШИЙ, ЩО КОЖЕН ЗВІР НА НЬОГО ХОЧЕ БУТИ СХОЖИЙ. ХТО КОСТЮМ БОРСУКА ОДЯГАЄ — НА НЕИМОВІРНЕ СВЯТО ПОТРАПЛЯЄ!

The Big Plenty and the Wee Tubby Sparsely

Designer
Lara Bispinck

Material
300gsm gray paper

Size
180mm x 250mm

Completion
2014

'The Big Plenty and the Wee Tubby Sparsely' (*Das Große Viel und das Kleine Dicke Wenig*) is about child poverty in Germany. Despite the fact that Germany is a developed country, many children live in poverty. The good friendship between the characters in the story is intended to help children understand that money is not the most important thing in life. The 200-page children's book is printed on 300gsm cream-colored paper and its compact size customized to make it easier for children to hold. There are two versions of the spine; one is a gray hardcover and the other has multi-colored stitching. The hand-drawn typography cover and aquarelle illustrations give the book a handmade character.

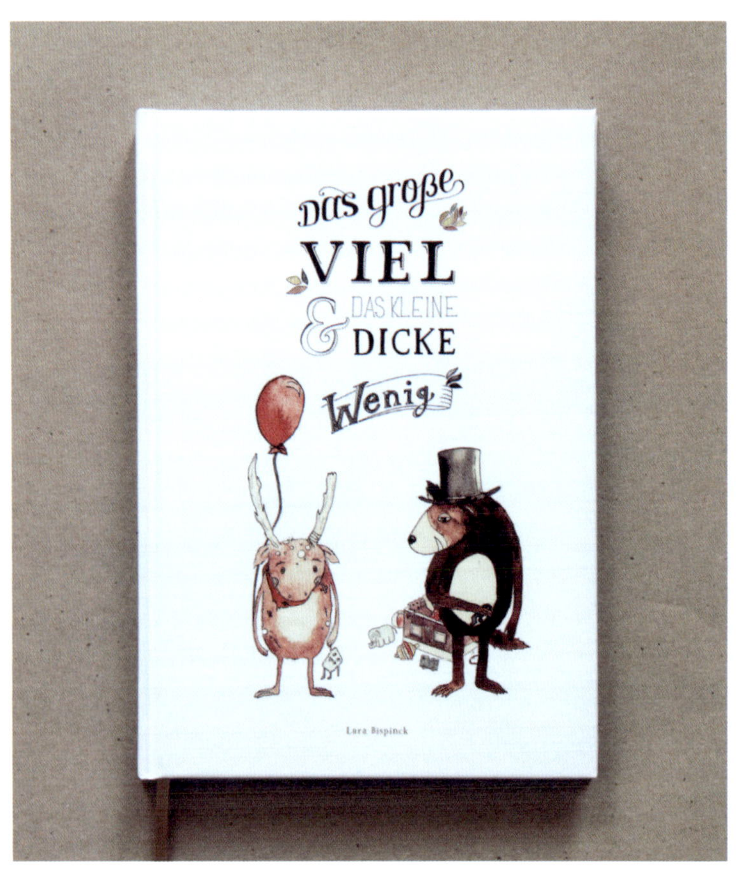

Zoe, Marina and Bo in the Country of Holey Plates

Authors
Ri Tori,
Olga Shitikova

Designer
Ri Tori

Size
210mm x 297mm

Completion
2015

This illustrated book by Ri Tori and Olga Shitikova is about food, imagination, and drawing. Food and ingredients become lands, clothing, flora, and fauna and lead readers on a journey of discovery and wonder. With illustrations and text spilling across the pages, readers will find hidden details each time they revisit the book.

КТО-ТО
ГДЕ
ВЫ
МОИ МОЛОЧНЫЕ
МАКАРОНЧИКИ
АУ
МОЛОКО
Уважаемый
Вы случайно
не встречали
кашу
манную?
Кого-то
ПОТЕРЯЛ
МОЖЕТ БЫТЬ
В ОКОШКЕ
В КАРМАНЕ

A Book About Tomorrow

Designer
Sevilya Nariman-qizi Ibrahimova

Material
160gsm matte paper

Size
140mm x 280mm

Completion
2014

Mixing illustrations, collages, and photography, 'A Book About Tomorrow' is a book, a story, and a game about the uncertainty of tomorrow. The book contains handmade color and black-and-white pencil illustrations and is supplemented by a collage of vintage illustrations. Each spread is different from the previous spread to convey the concept of uncertainty and diversity.

This book is a game with a labyrinth for readers to navigate. It has a hole that connects pages to one another and is intended to arouse readers' interest; while looking at one page of the book, readers can see an aspect of the next page. The typography combines three fonts—serif, Grotesque, and hand-made calligraphy based on children's curved writing—to create a playful aesthetic.

ЗНАЙТИ В ЛІСІ НЕБО, ЯКЕ ВВАЖАЄ, ЩО ВОНО ОЗЕРО

ЗІРКИ
сховаються
У
ШАФІ

МЕНЮ СНІДАНКА
ПЕРСИК
майже 2 шт.
АРТИШОК
хто зна як
його готувати
КАПУСТА
синього кольору
СМОРОДИНА
червона
(обожнюю її)
26.
ПОСНІДАТИ
У КОМПАНІЇ ВЕЛИЧЕЗНОГО ЗВІРА,
(який навіть у кухню не поміщається)
27.

ВСЕ
ВЗУТТЯ
СВІТУ
припинить
НАТИРАТИ
МОЗОЛІ
34.
35.

ЗАВТРА
ПОЧАТИ ДИВИТИСЬ
НЕЗВИЧАЙНИМ ПОГЛЯДОМ
НА ЗВИЧАЙНІ РЕЧІ

Кожен день ти бачиш, як тобі здається, звичайні нудні речі.

А вони аж нітрошечки не нудні, просто ти дивишся не під тим кутом, що треба.

Щоб подивитися незвичайним поглядом на звичайну річ, потрібно трохи нахилитися вперед і повернути голову на 25 градусів вправо.

25

Ось тут то ти і прозрієш! Тарілка з супом, виявляється, це головний убір з начінкою, а по вулицях розгулюють зебри туди і сюди. І як раніше ти цього не помічав?

38.
39.

ЗАВТРА
7
1
15
ПОЧАТИ
поважати
кожну частинку цього світу, якою маленькою вона б не здавалася б. Самим маленьким істотам планети так подобається, коли їм приділяють особливу увагу.
І ТЕБЕ ПОВАЖАЮ, ЛИСТИК
21.
2
ЗАВТРА
6
16.
3
поважаю тебе, комаха
Я ПОВАЖАЮ ТЕБЕ КОРАЛ
8
62.
63.

Adventure in the Meadow Rhön

Designer
Maria Martin

Material
300gsm and 250gsm matte,
white coated paper

Size
100mm x 100mm

Completion
2013

'Adventure in the Meadow Rhön' is the first book in a 10-issue anthology by Maria Martin. The story is about three friends embarking on a wonderful and exciting adventure when they discover the unique nature of the Rhön—a nature reserve in Thuringia, Germany.

Intended for children aged three to seven years old, the main themes of the book are healthy food, nature, and the Rhön meadow, with content on organic farming, traditions, conservation, species protection, and handmade products. The compact format of this book is designed for children's small hands. The Scala Sans and Syntax typefaces are very clear in 13.5pt font size. The multi-colored and saturated illustrations are freehand and colored digitally.

Diese steckten sie sich dann genüsslich in den Mund. Was war das? Es musste etwas sehr feines und leckeres sein. Nach einiger Zeit schauten sich die Kinder prüfend um, dann beugten sie sich nach unten zu einem alten dicken Baumstamm. Er war schon morsch und hohl.
Dort hinein legten sie die wundersamen Dinge und verdeckten das Loch mit ein paar Grasbüscheln. Tabsi beobachtete aufgeregt wie die Menschenkinder ausgelassen zurück ins Dorf schlenderten. Was hatten
Von nun an kam sie jeden Tag zu dem Versteck und probierte von den verschiedensten Süßigkeiten. Einige der Leckereien waren so hart, dass man sie nur lutschen konnte, andere waren mit einer weißen oder dunklen Crème gefüllt.
Abends hatte sie dann oft keinen Appetit... frisch gekochten Blütenbrei ihrer Mutter. Sogar der Apfelnachtisch oder die frisch geernteten Waldbeeren schmeckten ihr nicht mehr so gut... Bevor sie zu dem Versteck flog war sie immer... sehr aufgeregt und hoffte, dass noch genug... Naschen da war. Nach dem Zuckerschmaus leg- te sie sich auf das kühle Moos, ruhte sich aus...

Kiku and Anamitra

Designer
Anna Falcó

Size
200mm x 200mm

Completion
2015

The main character of this book is based on a boy Anna Falcó met while volunteering in Nepal. In the story the boy meets a hawk (the designer's family name Falcó means 'hawk' in Spanish) that has no friends because his very large wings scare people. The boy and the hawk become friends and the hawk uses his large wings to fly to Barcelona and bring the boy's sister to visit Nepal.

The designer balances contrasting colors and techniques with composition. Falcó employed a standard illustrated book format and used Futura typeface for its geometric proportions and clean, modern style that contrasts with the handmade illustrations. Although planning to make the book very colorful—like Nepal—in the end Falcó used black-and-white illustrations to represent the story as a memory with touches of color to express inner revelation.

Hi havia una vegada un nen que vivia
en un poble molt bonic,
rodejat de verds camps d'arròs
i de frondosa selva.

Un diumenge pel matí, com sempre feia, havia baixat
al riu a banyar-se i mentre s'estava ensabonant va
sentir entre els matolls, una veueta que el saludava.
En Kiku es va espantar però no va fer-ne cas,
pensant que estava mig adormit i
que encara somiava.
Tanmateix, la veueta va continuar
preguntant-li si volia ser el seu amic.

En Kiku tot i tenir molta por va ser valent,
tal com els seus pares haurien volgut
i es va atrevir a acostar-se als matolls.

Words to the Point

Designer
Monika Grubizna

Material
Cover: 300gsm Serixo
Leaves: 150gsm Amber Graphic

Printing Technology
Spot varnish

Size
190mm x 240mm

Completion
2014

Publisher
Ethnographic Museum

'Words to the Point' explains the meaning of classic Polish proverbs and phrases. Each illustration depicts an object in the collection of the Ethnographic Museum in Kraków and is accompanied by the meaning of the relevant proverb. The book's aim is to describe the function of a selection of obsolete objects and explain the expressions associated with them.

The book is intended to bring children and adults together to read and share their knowledge and experience. The book is laid out in alphabetical order and the back cover doubles as a space for children's activities, such as drawing objects, making notes, and writing letters.

NIEDŹWIEDZIA PRZYSŁUGA

Niedźwiedź kiedyś nazywał się zupełnie inaczej, ale ponieważ ze strachu przed nim nie wymieniano jego imienia, dawno już zapomniano, jak ono brzmiało. Wiedziano, że lubi miód, więc mówiono o nim zjadacz miodu, czyli „miedźwiedź", a potem niedźwiedź. Żeby przezwyciężyć lęk, próbowano też trochę ośmieszyć niedźwiedzia. Wytykano mu ociężałość i niezgrabność. [Sk]ąd zatem pomysł, żeby spodziewać się od niego przysługi?

[Otó]ż to!

[Nie]dźwiedzia przysługa to pomoc udzielona [nie] w porę, przynosząca szkodę.

Zwrot pochodzi z bajki o pewnym pustelniku, który żył w przyjaźni z niedźwiedziem. Wszystko podobno dobrze się układało, dopóki niedźwiedź nie zabił śpiącego współlokatora uderzeniem łapy. Nie zrobił tego specjalnie. Chciał tylko troskliwie spędzić muchę z jego czoła...

W dziedzinie sprytnego wykorzystania sił przyrody dawne młyny mogłyby konkurować z dzisiejszymi elektrowniami wiatrowymi. Do poruszania urządzeń, które przerabiały twarde ziarno na puszystą mąkę, wykorzystywano **energię wiatru albo wody**.

Żeby woda płynęła mocniejszym strumieniem, budowano tamy na rzece, dwupoziomowe stawy lub stawiano młyn w miejscu, gdzie można było skorzystać z nachylenia terenu – płynąca wartko woda wprawiała w ruch zanurzone w niej młyńskie koło, a ono pociągało za sobą cały mechanizm wewnątrz młyna.

Powiedzenie „woda na młyn" oznacza, że ktoś znalazł się w korzystnej sytuacji, chociaż właściwie nie ma w tym jego zasługi.

Być może wynika ono trochę z zazdrości, że komuś aż tak się [pow]odzi. Młynarze byli jednymi [z naj]bogatszych mieszkańców w [... Zara]biali nie tylko na mieleniu [mąk]i, ale też na sprzedaży [ryb] hodowanych w stawach [przy]młynnych, wytwarzaniu k[...] [ol]ejów, wyrabianiu słodu do [piwa]. Hodowali także zwierzęt[a], [któ]rym bardzo smakowały [odp]ady z przerabianego w mł[ynie] [zbo]ża. Ale czy to wszystko jes[t] [rze]czywiście tylko [...]gą w[...]

KTO SIĘ CZUBI, TEN SIĘ LUBI

Czy można jeść mało jak wróbelek? Chodzić gęsiego? Chować ze strachu głowę w piach jak struś? Wiele spośród naszych zachowań opisujemy poprzez odniesienie do świata ptaków. Także to, kiedy zaczepiamy lubianą osobę, żeby zwrócić na siebie jej uwagę. Żartobliwe docinki, psikusy i płatanie figli nazywamy czubieniem.

Porównanie do czubiących się ptaków wzięło się z obserwacji walczących kogutów. Bijące się o pozycję na podwórku koguty dziobią się po czubach, czyli czerwonych grzebieniach wyrastających na czubkach ich głów. Stąd też dawniej o wszczynaniu kłótni czy bójki mówiono – „iść z kimś w czuby". Dziś określenie to ma przewrotne znaczenie.

SMALIĆ CHOLEWKI

Dawniej skórzane buty były bardzo drogie. Nie każdego było na nie stać, a jeśli już udało się je kupić, wkładano je tylko na specjalne okazje. W trosce o ich ładny wygląd oraz dobry stan, buty nacierano **sadzą zmieszaną ze smalcem** (wyobrażasz sobie?!). Czynność tę nazywano smoleniem. Dzięki niej buty czerniały i nabierały połysku. Podobny efekt dawało smalenie, które polegało na **opalaniu butów nad ogniem.** Przechadzając się w takich butach, można było zrobić wrażenie. Gdy kawaler zabiegał o względy swojej wybranki, robił wszystko, by wyglądać elegancko. Czernił więc wysokie cholewki butów.

To dlatego, gdy dziś mówimy, że ktoś smoli lub smali cholewki, mamy na myśli, że się zaleca, przymila, darzy ukochaną osobę szczególną uwagą.

32

TRAFIŁA KOSA NA KAMIEŃ

Kosa wygląda trochę groźnie: długie, zakrzywione ostrze osadzone wysoko na długim drewnianym trzonku. Lepiej omijać ją z daleka. Potrafi ostro i bezwzględnie poczynać sobie z łanami zboża i z trawą. Jednym zamaszystym ruchem robi niezłe spustoszenie. Wszystko idzie dobrze, dopóki nie okaże się, że wśród wiotkich źdźbeł, kruchych łodyg i wątłych kwiatów kryje się twardy, ciężki kamień. Jeśli ostrze kosy trafi na kamień, może się okazać, że nie wyjdzie z tego cało.

Niespodziewany opór kamienia wobec zwycięskiego pochodu kosy przypomina, że nawet taka ostra sztuka może trafić na godnego siebie przeciwnika. Z im większą siłą na niego natrze, tym mocniej się wyszczerbi.

53

y wóz konny
żenia z pola
ziemniaków.
zwykle był
doczny z oddali
iętrzyły się ponad
Aby nie wypadły,
burtami, czyli
ami w postaci
lub drabin.

Dziś nie tak łatwo spotkać f
Wozy ciągnięte przez konie
i przyczepami. Nadal jedna
że mamy czegoś bardzo du
„fura" odnoszącego się do

Fura oznacza zatem

masę, niezliczoną il

O furze czego marz

JEDNO KOPYTO

zybierać postać
ewcy kształtowali
zoru – kopyta.
rma w kształcie
kowo **dla**
a. To dlatego
mówiono, że
złowiek ma
dodatek różne.

Aby dopasować buty, a ponadto sprawić, żeby były cieplejsze, ludzie wyściełali je słomą. Samą stopę owijali zaś onucą, czyli lnianym bądź flanelowym kawałkiem materiału (zimą był to najczęściej materiał wełniany).

43

How to Deal With Monsters

Author
Daniela Zbytovská

Designer
Barbora Klimszová

Illustrator
Karolína Stryková

Printing Technology
Spot color, debossing

Size
225mm x 225mm

Completion
2014

'How to Deal With Monsters,' written by actress Daniela Zbytovská, illustrated by Karolína Stryková, and designed by Barbora Klimszová, is a compilation of six inspiring stories for children based on the experiences of adults. The book is designed to be interactive for children and adults with revision sheets at the end of each story to remind readers of important moments and to encourage children to ask questions.

The Avenir typeface is used throughout the book with reported speech in a bolder, larger font and narrative in a regular, smaller font. The designer used the big, bold font for reported clauses in order to focus attention on characters' communication and to make it easier for readers to concentrate on significant moments in the story.

Čert je prostě čert! Co si budeme povídat! Dělá čertoviny a kouká, jak by koho zkazil a odnesl do pekla! Není v něm pranic dobrého. Možná jenom docela malá dušička, co je tak malá, že by se protáhla klíčovou dírkou.

Toník se čertů bál. Když byl sám doma, zavřel veliké dveře od domu, zamkl je na dva západy, lehl si do postele a přikryl se velikánskou peřinou, takže pod ní ani nebyl vidět.

Někdy se mu zdálo, že někdo cizí kouká oknem do ložnice, jindy že někdo klepe na dveře. Často se stávalo, že když ho potom ráno maminka vedla do školky, našel před domem malou hromádku uhlí.

„Čert nikdy nespí!"

říkával tatínek a byla to pravda. Jednou, bylo to ve čtvrtek večer, když maminka s tatínkem odešli jako každý čtvrtek k sousedům hrát piškvorky, Toník dobře zamkl dveře a chystal se hupsnout pod peřinu. Vtom zaslechl trojí zabouchání na dveře. A za chvíli zase trojí zabouchání a po chvilce opět trojí

bušení. Třikrát tři je devět… devět zabouchání, to nevěští nic dobrého. Toníkovi ztuhla krev v žilách, ale pak si řekl, že tady asi žádný strach nepomůže, a odvážně se zeptal: **„Kdo je?"**

„Jak kdo je?" ozvalo se za dveřmi.

„Otvírej! Jsem čert a zrovinka dneska jsem se rozhodl, že tě naučím nějaký pořádný čertoviny! No, uznej, Toníku, máte tady na zemi strašlivou nudu! Žádná zábava už tu není!

Čert aby se tu unudil k smrti. A víš proč? Víš ty, Toníku, proč?

Protože děti už dneska neumějí pořádně zlobit! Jo, dřív, to bejvávaly časy! Děcka zlobila a já je vesele odnášel do pekla! Pokaždé, šestého prosince, v den svatého Mikuláše jsem si odnášel plný pytel zlobivých dětí k nám do

Vzala si hřebínek, pěkně si učesala vlásky, aby šla na návštěvu hezky upravená, hřebínek strčila do kapsy a vypravila se za čarodějnicí.
Šla hustým, tmavým lesem, asi tak dva kilometry, možná i víc, až uviděla ten nejvyšší strom a na něm chýši, zavěšenou jako veliké ptačí hnízdo.
„Haloooo, paní, jste tam?" zavolala Anička pevným hláskem.
Z chýše se ozvalo zachrochtnutí, potom mlasknutí a nakonec se vyklonila nečesaná hlava. Z černých očí jí šlehaly plameny zlosti. **„Co tady chceš?**

Kliď se odsud!"

zaskřehotala hlava.
„Přišla jsem si s vámi promluvit," řekla Anička a ze sluje se ozval hurónský smích. Baba se smála, až šišky ze stromů padaly a ptáci vylekaně z hnízd vylétali.

„Cože? Co je to za povedený vtip! Řekni to ještě jednou!"

zařvala baba.

„Chci si s vámi promluvit, paní, prosím!"

zopakovala svoji prosbu Anička.
Baba se přestala smát a zasyčela:

„Cssss… Tak takovou drzost jsem ještě nezažila, a to jsem na světě sto padesát let! No, dobrá, jak chceš!"

pochopit, že když někoho násilím zavře pod pokličku, tak si s ním nebude hrát, i kdyby se postavil na hlavu!
„Tak poslouchej, ty nádhero zelená," povídá Sebík, „to ti nedošlo, že když chceš kamarády, tak je nemůžeš násilím držet pod pokličkou? To dá rozum, že takhle si s tebou hrát nikdy nebudou.

Pusť je na svobodu, a uvidíš!"

Hastrman se vyděsil: **„Čo?**

Já je puštím a žůštanu úplně šám!"
„Pusť je, a uvidíš!"

řekl Sebík.

„Sám jsi tak jako tak! Nemáš co ztratit!"

„Aha, nemám čo žtlatit," řekl hastrman a zmizel pod hladinou. Rychle začal odkrývat pokličky a z hrnečků postupně vyplavávaly ztracené děti. Mezi nimi i Maruška Horáková a Pepíček Polák, který hned volal na Sebíka:

„Sebo, co tam sedíš, ať už jsi ve vodě!"

Kluci křičeli, holky pištěly a hastrman celý ožil a pištěl a křičel s nimi.
Křik dětí od rybníka probudil celou vesnici. Jako první se vzbudil Sebíkův táta, běžel do garáže a zvolal:

„Někdo mi ukradl žebřík! To je nadělení, to je nadělení! Co když ho teď budu potřebovat!"

A tak se večer na mýtince sešla úplně celá třída. Vůbec nikdo nechyběl, takže tam stálo dvacet dětí a zíralo na paní učitelku. Paní učitelka z toho byla chvilku vyvedená z míry, ale potom se vzpamatovala, seřadila děti do dvojstupu a vyrazili do lesa.
Ivánek Charvát měl s sebou dokonce i svačinu a drze se smál paní učitelce za zády.

„No teda, viděl jsem toho už dost, ale takhle bláznivou učitelku ještě ne!"

Šli asi tak osm minut, když vtom se ozvalo:

„Húúúúúú… búúúúúúúú!"

Ivánkovi Charvátovi zaskočil chleba v krku, tak se lekl. Celá třída se chtěla dát na útěk, ale paní učitelka zapískala na píšťalku a zavelela: **„Klid, děti, klid, nemáme se čeho bát, je nás i se mnou dvacet jedna a on je sám."** Ve skutečnosti jich bylo jenom dvacet, protože Ivánek Charvát se ukryl do houští a tam se strachy celý třásl.
Strašidlo najednou povídá: **„Dovolte, abych se představil, húúúúúú… jsem Hubert… lesní strašidlo. „Dvořáková,"** řekla paní učitelka a podala strašidlu ruku.
A pak se představila postupně celá třída kromě Ivánka Charváta.

Little Wolf and
the Wind,
Water and Sun

Designer
Thùy Cốm

Size
200mm x 200mm

Completion
2013

Publisher
Room to Read

'Little Wolf and the Wind, Water and Sun' is a story about a little wolf that tired of being cast in the same old stories created his own. The book begins in black and white to reflect the mundane story and various colors are introduced as he escapes into his own colorful tale. A large serif font is intended to make reading easier and the color of the letters sometimes changes with the narrative of the story. Silhouettes at the page corners appear animated when the reader quickly flips the leaves of the book.

Room to Read works in collaboration with local communities, partner organizations, and governments to develop literacy skills and reading habits through a Grade 1 and 2 phonics-based instruction program, library, and picture books.

Mấy chuyện chó sói này cũ mèm rồi!
Con sẽ tìm câu chuyện ĐÁNG KỂ NHẤT ngoài kia!

Câu chuyện của tớ
sẽ thật nhiều màu!
Làm thế nào
ra được ngoài kia?
Hỏi gió ấy!
Chúng tớ chỉ ở trong nhà,
chẳng đi đâu xa.

Life of Pigeons

Designer
Emma Perrin

Material
90gsm Cyclus recycled paper

Size
105mm x 200mm

Completion
2015

Photo Credit
Graeme Perrin

'Life of Pigeons' (*Dueliv*) is a brochure for children to obtain general knowledge about pigeons and learn to differentiate five breeds of pigeons that inhabit Denmark's cities and countryside. Emma Perrin's intention was to make the facts simple and entertaining and able to be easily read and understood.

The brochure is intended as a teaching supplement to make learning fun for children and educators. Illustrations are in black ink and the birds are acrylic painted. Each pigeon is presented in characteristic colors accompanied by relevant information and a short comic strip depicting a scene from its life.

Livet som ringdue
JO... LAD OS TAGE OVER TIL FRU HANSEN I NR 7... HUN HANDLER I IRMA
ER DER IK' LIDT FOR MEGET SALT I DET HER...?

KU-KU-KUU, KÅ-KÅ
KU-KU-KUU, KÅ-KÅ
KU-KU-KUU, KÅ-KÅ
RINGDUEN
DRRO - DRRO - DRROO
DRRO - DRRO - DRROO
TURTELDUEN
KUU-KU
KUU-KU
KUU-KU
HULDUEN
DO - DOO-DO
DO - DOO-DO
KURRR
KURRR
BYDUEN
TYRKERDUEN
DE 5 DUEARTER SOM LEVER FRIT I DANMARK

OM DUEN OG YNGEL
FODRING MED DUEMÆLK
KRO
LÆGGER CA 2 ÆG, SOM ER HVIDE
UNGERNE PASSES AF BEGGE FORÆLDRE. FORLADER REDEN EFTER 3-4 UGER
DUEN HAR EN UDPOSNING AF SPISERØRET KALDET EN "KRO", OPMAGASINERER FØDE
UNGERNE FODRES I DE FØRSTE DAGE MED "DUEMÆLK", EN OSTEAGTIG SEKRET FRA "KROEN", SOM ER FEDT/PROTEIN RIG
PARRENE YNGLER ADSKILT OPRETHOLDER TERRITORIER
REDEN ER SPINKEL MEN SOLID

RINGDUEN
STOR · 38-43 CM
HVID PLET PÅ HALSEN
HVIDT BÅND OVER VINGEN
FINDES I HAVER, BYPARKER OFTE VED FODERBRÆT
SKY I SKOVEN OG VED ÅBENT LAND
I JAGTSÆSONEN SKYDES CA 300.000 RINGDUER HVER ÅR
KALDES OGSÅ FOR "SKOVDUE"
MEST ALMINDELIGE DANSKE DUE

HULduen
LILLE • 28-32 CM
BLÅGRÅ • SKY

BOR I SKOVEN
I NORD/ØST JYLLAND OG ØER
CA 800-1000 PAR I DK

BOR I HULLER I TRÆER
I KANINHULLER
FORLADTE RÆVEGRAVE
KLITOMRÅDER

ER FREDET

TURTELDUER
TÆNK AT FOLK IKKE VED VI EKSISTERER...
JA- DET ER FORDI VI ER SÅ SJÆLDNE...
TURRR... TURRR... TURRR... TURAR...
OG SPECIELLE...!

Grandma Bice Tells

Authors
Guglielmo Donzella, Sonia Tri

Designer
Anna Antonutti

Illustrators
Anna Antonutti, Elena Blasi,
Eva Disilvestro, Simona Ermacora,
Monica Fabris, Chiara Giorgiutti,
Michela Giorgiutti, Sonja Monaca,
Sarolta Szulyovszky,
Nina Andrea Van Eeden

Material
Fedrigoni Arcoprint paper

Size
280mm x 280mm

Completion
2013

'Grandma Bice Tells' (*Nonna Bice Racconta*) is an illustrated book of stories and legends hailing from the Friuli Venezia Giulia region of Italy. The ten stories written by Guglielmo Donzella and Sonia Tri are accompanied by the work of ten illustrators, each expressing their own style and techniques.

While this book is for children, the stories are also intended to encourage grandparents to revisit their childhood. For this reason, the title font, warm color palette, and graphic layout are designed like an old school exercise book. The cover illustration has a rural atmosphere with children gathered around a fire listening to stories while their grandmother stitches a crochet blanket.

La Principessa di Poffabro

Racconto di **Sonia Tri**
Illustrazioni di **Monica Fabris**

Tra i maestosi boschi della Val Colvera, sulle pendici delle Alpi Carniche, proprio dove scorre il fiume che dà il nome alla vallata, sorge Poffabro, un borgo piccolo e tranquillo.
Tutto il paese è attraversato da pittoresche viuzze e piazzette dove si affacciano le case di pietra bianca con i davanzali dei balconi colmi di fiori. La fama della sua bellezza è dovuta anche alla sua piazza in cui si può ammirare la grande fontana, ed alla maestria dei suoi abitanti nel lavorare il ferro battuto.
Questo luogo era conosciuto fin dai tempi più remoti, varcando i confini della vallata e raggiungendo le terre più lontane.
Fu così che un ricco sultano, venuto a sapere della sua esistenza, decise di recarsi in visita, con l'intento di farsi costruire una bella spada.
Gli abitanti del posto, appresa la novità, si radunarono tutti attorno alla piccola fontana della piazza, orgogliosi di tale scelta, ma timorosi di non essere all'altezza di tale compito, considerato il fatto che dovevano accontentare niente meno che un sultano!
Essi si sapevano lavorare il ferro, ma non erano certo abituati ad ospitare nessuno in quei luoghi, dove gli unici suoni che si udivano erano il festoso cinguettare degli uccelli e il laborioso "tin-tun, tin-tun" delle incudini e martelli che usciva dalle botteghe.
- Se è un sultano avrà anche un esercito! - disse il primo fabbro. - Esatto! Allora gli costruiremo le sciabole più belle del mondo! - prosegui il secondo fabbro e, alla fine, tutti convennero che quello sarebbe stato il lavoro più bello e adeguato per un sovrano.

che se ne stava tutto il giorno chiuso nella sua officina a battere il ferro, senza mai socializzare con nessuno.
Infatti era tanto bravo quanto odioso, e nulla destava la sua attenzione al di fuori del suo lavoro; nemmeno l'arrivo del sultano!
Affrontare Nane non era facile; era molto meglio avere a che fare con un orso nel bosco piuttosto che con lui. Come fare, dunque, per ottenere la sua collaborazione?
- Potrei provarci io... - disse una fanciulla facendosi varco tra tutti i fabbri.
Era Elvira, la figlia di Nane, una ragazza delicata e dolce, l'unica che avrebbe ottenuto attenzione dal padre.
Fu così che a fine giornata, quando padre e figlia si trovarono attorno al tavolo per la cena, lei lo pregò di costruire la preziosa spada.
Il vecchio allora le disse: - Va bene figlia mia, costruirò la spada più bella che un re possa desiderare, ma tu devi promettermi che non mi chiederai mai più nulla per un lunghissimo tempo! -.
Elvira fece la sua promessa e Nane iniziò il suo capolavoro.
Trascorsero alcuni mesi e a Poffabro tutto era pronto per l'arrivo del sultano.
Le ragazze del borgo, nel frattempo, si erano confezionate le "scarpètis", caratteristiche pantofoline in velluto nero interamente cucite a mano, per danzare al suo ricevimento.
Solo Elvira, non potendo chiedere più nulla al padre, era l'unica del paese a non averne, dovendo così rinunciare a partecipare al ballo che si sarebbe tenuto in onore del sultano.
Arrivò così il giorno tanto atteso e tutti gli abitanti del borgo accolsero i nuovi ospiti organizzando, in loro onore, una bellissima festa.
Solo Elvira, dopo aver promesso al padre di non chiedergli più nulla, si ritrovò senza le scarpette nuove e senza il permesso di partecipare al ballo.
Il vecchio Nane però, che tanto l'amava, si sentì in colpa e di notte mentre tutti dormivano riuscì a preparare, col fil di ferro e qualche rimanenza di filigrana d'oro, un bellissimo paio di scarpètis per la sua Elvira.
Il giorno dopo la figlia non credeva ai suoi occhi! Indossò quelle calzature ed andò ad accogliere il sultano con le amiche del paese. Tuttavia quelle pantofole erano molto

scomode e le provocavano un dolore così acuto da doverle togliere e rimanere scalza e sanguinante davanti a tutti.
Il suo disagio e il suo imbarazzo erano enormi ma il sultano, ammirato ugualmente dalla sua grazia, le chiese comunque di ballare, anche se lei si rifiutava per la vergogna di essere scalza.
- La dignità di una principessa non è nei suoi piedi, ma nel suo cuore - disse a gran voce il sultano stringendo la ragazza a sé.
Ballarono così tutta la notte e Poffabro, il piccolo borgo della Val Colvera illuminato da mille fiaccole accese, era ancora più suggestivo e per una notte ebbe anche la sua principessa, come un vero reame incantato tra i boschi.

La leggenda del Ponte del Diavolo

Racconto popolare
Illustrazioni di **Chiara Giorgiutti**

Molto tempo fa, nella bella città di Cividale, gli abitanti del luogo erano costretti a fare lunghi giri per raggiungere i quartieri e le frazioni del loro borgo.
Il paese, infatti, era attraversato da un alto burrone, sulle cui sponde si affacciavano le case e gli orti. Sotto scorreva il torrente Natisone.
Questo fiume era assai prezioso e, grazie alla limpidezza delle sue acque, gli abitanti di Cividale potevano irrigare i campi, riempire i pozzi, lavare i panni, abbeverare i loro animali.
I collegamenti tra le due alte sponde erano assicurati da tremolanti passerelle costruite con corde e legno e gli animali, al seguito dei loro padroni, non potevano neppure salirvi.
Nacque, quindi, il desiderio di costruire un nuovo ponte, fatto di pietre e cemento, solido e possente, capace di resistere alla forza del fiume in piena ed a tutte le intemperie.
I cividalesi, aiutati dagli abitanti dei paesi vicini, più volte intrapresero l'opera, ma ogni volta avversità naturali e crolli improvvisi rendevano vano ogni tentativo e molti cominciarono a pensare che era il Diavolo in persona a non volere quella costruzione.
Il parroco, allora, iniziò a celebrare molte messe con la speranza di allontanare la presenza del Maligno, senza però ottenere alcun risultato.

Arrivarono molti forestieri richiamati da questo fatto e tutti promettevano soluzioni miracolose, senza mai riuscire nel loro intento.
I paesani, intanto, di fronte all'ennesima rovina del cantiere si erano quasi tutti rassegnati ad abbandonare l'idea quando un giorno si presentò a loro un vecchio santo eremita il quale si propose di risolvere per sempre la questione.
Ritiratosi in una grotta poco distante aspettò la visita del Demonio. Poco dopo, infatti, egli non tardò ad arrivare confessando di essere il responsabile dei danni provocati.
Accettò la proposta di essere lui a costruire il ponte, ma come compenso chiese di poter portare all'inferno il primo essere che lo avesse attraversato.
Tutti gli abitanti, riunitisi in assemblea con il loro podestà ascoltarono la proposta ed accettarono, seppure un po' spaventati, l'offerta del Demonio.

Scesa la notte il Diavolo si mise al lavoro e, per non avere curiosi attorno a sé, scatenò un terribile temporale tanto da costringere anche i più coraggiosi a rimanere nelle loro case. E tra lampi, tuoni, e una pioggia battente per tutta la notte lavorò alla costruzione del nuovo ponte.
Al mattino, finita la tempesta, gli abitanti uscirono dalle loro case dirigendosi là dove sorgeva la nuova costruzione e tutti rimasero incantati nell'ammirare la grande opera e si resero conto che solo il Diavolo in persona avrebbe potuto fare una meraviglia così.
A questo punto, però, iniziò a diffondersi la terribile idea di dover sorteggiare la persona che, per prima, avrebbe dovuto attraversare il ponte.

Scese un silenzio di tomba tra i presenti, interrotto da un coro di grida proveniente dalla piazza del duomo.
Era un gruppo di ragazzi intenti a correre dietro un cane. Quest'ultimo, per scappare dai monelli, si fece un varco tra la folla prendendo la direzione del ponte.
Ad aspettare, in mezzo alla costruzione in pietra, c'era il Diavolo con un sacco aperto tra le mani e, non potendo fare altro, fu costretto a rinchiudervi il povero animale.
Si rese conto, allora, della grande beffa ricevuta e, carico di rabbia ed in preda ad un'ira feroce, trasformò il sacco in una grande pietra, gettandola sul greto del fiume.
Ancora oggi quel grande masso è lì, visibile a tutti, per ricordare questa storia andata a lieto fine grazie soprattutto al sacrificio di quella povera bestiola.

Scesa in cucina la vecchietta si mise subito all'opera. Circondata dagli animaletti che la osservavano curiosi e pieni di entusiasmo disse loro:

- Siete stati proprio gentili e di buon cuore. Per premiarvi e per fare una bella sorpresa alla mia nipotina, preparerò un dolce in ricordo di Guba. Con questo gesto non la riporteremo più tra noi, ma la ricorderemo con l'affetto e l'amore che merita -.

Terminata la cottura, mentre il dolce usciva dal forno, tutti rimasero incantati. La sua forma era uguale a quella di Guba quando si accoccolava felice accanto a Ilaria e non vi fu gioia più grande quando la bambina, svegliata dai rumori che salivano dalla cucina, scese le scale e vide sulla tavola, circondata dai suoi amichetti, una torta uguale alla sua amata micetta.

Da quel giorno Ilaria comprese che la sua gattina Guba non sarebbe più ritornata con lei e a nulla sarebbero serviti i suoi pianti, solo a rendere più tristi gli amichetti che adesso le rimanevano vicini.

E in onore di Guba, Ilaria decise di chiamare il dolce fatto dalla nonna "Gubana", in ricordo di quel micio così tenero e affettuoso, ma anche così dolce...

Refolino e la storia del Carso Collio

Racconto popolare rivisto da **Guglielmo Donzella**
Illustrazioni di **Michela Giorgiutti**

Care bambine, cari bambini, voglio darvi il mio affettuoso e svolazzante benvenuto. Mi chiamo Refolino, il venticello che non riesce mai a stare fermo, che muove le foglie degli alberi, fa dondolare dolcemente i fili d'erba e porta un po' di fresco sollievo nelle calde e afose giornate d'estate.

Ah, dimenticavo, no... non sono io quello che soffia forte d'inverno, no... quella è mia nonna, la Bora, che quando si arrabbia... fa venire i brividi a tutti e non sono nemmeno quello che, ogni tanto, s'infila tra tuoni, lampi e scrosci di pioggia, no... lui è mio nonno Eolone, sempre di cattivo umore, un caratteraccio...

Io sono buono... e siccome sono un gran curiosone oggi voglio portarvi in un angolo pittoresco del Friuli Venezia Giulia: sul Carso e sul Collio e raccontarvi la loro storia. Dovete sapere che quando Dio, creando la Terra, si soffermò in questi territori fece delle belle montagne per riparare la pianura friulana dai venti freddi del nord. Ma le montagne cominciarono a protestare perché volevano essere alte come quelle vicino alla Svizzera.

Il Signore, mosso da quella strana richiesta, chiese all'Arcangelo Gabriele di procurare altre pietre e portarle verso i monti della Carnia e delle Alpi Giulie.

Ma, si sa, il diavolo dispettoso ci mise del suo e con tutta la sua forza riuscì a bucare i sacchi colmi di pietre trasportati dall'angelo. Alcune caddero vicino il mare (e non potete immaginare il fracasso che fecero!), altre rotolarono verso i monti.

A quel punto il povero angelo fu preso da un grande sconforto. Mai avrebbe immaginato che il diavolo arrivasse ad essere così impertinente e dispettoso!

Il Signore, commosso da quella triste vicenda, si rivolse così al suo fedele servitore:

- Non ti preoccupare. Per premiarti del tuo lavoro trasformerò le pietre vicino il mare in candide e pittoresche scogliere che si immergeranno nelle acque blu del golfo. In quelle accanto creerò affascinanti grotte impreziosite da tante bellissime stalattiti e attraversate da fiumi sotterranei. Più a nord, invece, ricoprirò le pietre rimaste con tanti ordinati e colorati filari di viti che pian

The Golden Egg

Designer
Emil Goozairow

Material
Luxury paper,
cardboard, polymer clay,
rope, hook

Size
50mm x 50mm

Completion
2015

'The Golden Egg' (*Das Goldene Ei*) is a German children's book that adapts a Russian fairy tale about a hen that laid a golden egg. Emil Goozairow wrote a new version of this fairy tale, painted the illustrations, and made several design options and bindings.

The book has a very unique structure with disclosed and extendible pop-ups, almost like origami. The linen cover has a medieval feel with metallic decoration made from polymer clay and a hook and rope clasp. This book is intended for children seven years of age or older.

Der Opa nahm das Ei:
Nanu! Die Eierschale ist wirklich
golden. Ist da ein Dotter drin?
wunderte sich der Opa. Da begann er
mit dem goldenen Ei vorsichtig auf
den Eichentisch zu klopfen. Er klopfte
und klopfte und hielt es gegen das
Licht und versuchte es mit dem
Taschenmesser zu öffnen. Da entglitt
das goldene Ei seinen Händen und fiel
auf den Boden ... statt
entzweizubrechen öffnete es sich. Zu
zwei gleichen Teilen ist es gegangen.
Im Handumdrehen erschienen aus
dem goldenen Ei mechanische
Figürchen mit Stäbchen, Rädchen und
Spiralchen, die sich seltsam zu
bewegen und zu transformieren
begannen. Eine schöne Musik setzte
ein und eine Vorstellung fing an.

Der Opa und die Oma
saßen bewegungslos und sahen die
Vorstellung über einen braven Ritter und
seine schöne Geliebte, über einen bösen
feuerspeienden Drachen, über einen
gerechten König und seinen miesen
Diener, der ihn verriet. Da kamen und
gingen aus der goldenen Eierschale
silberne, hölzerne, filigrane,
handgeschnitzte, bemalte und mit der
Emaille geschmückte Figürchen. Eine
Augenweide! Da war die Vorstellung zu
Ende, die Figürchen verschwanden in die
goldene Eierschale und die zwei gleichen
Eierteile gingen zusammen.

Der Opa und die Oma weinten,
weil sie diese wunderschöne Vorstellung
weiter sehen wollten. Und Rjaba saß in
ihrem Körbchen auf dem Fensterbrett und
gackerte.

Nancy Knows

Designer
Cybèle Young

Printing Technology
UV varnish

Size
254mm x 254mm

Completion
2014

Publisher
Tundra Books

Nancy Knows is a playful reminder that sometimes you have to let go to tap in. Nancy can remember all manner of things in a variety of ways including with her ears, her stomach, and even her heart. But Nancy knows she's forgotten something, she just can't remember what. Each spread of this whimsical picture book features images of intricate three-dimensional sculptures contained within expressive line art.

And forwards.

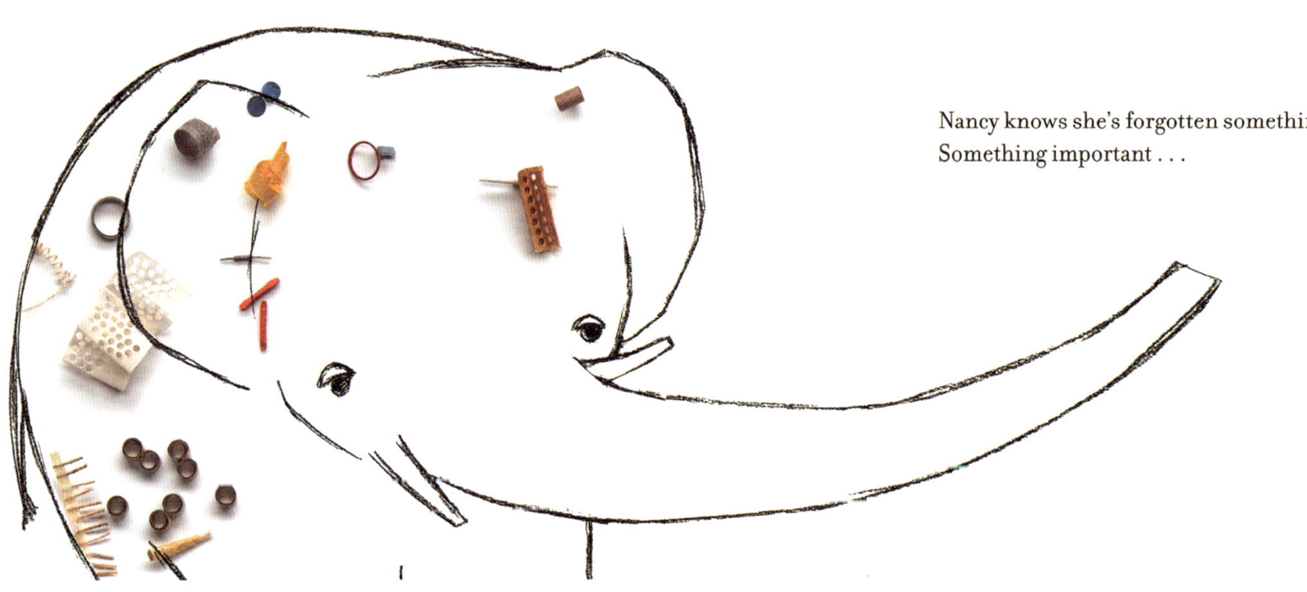

Nancy knows she's forgotten something. Something important . . .

She remembers things she knows . . .
Things with wheels.

Things like clothes.

Places to relax.

And places to go.

she thinks of all kinds of other things.
Often when Nancy tries to remember,

And her heart remembers things from all different places,
all kinds of times and all sorts of spaces.

Night Night Baby Heart

Author
Lenka Mikovcova

Designer
Vêra Ema Tataro

Size
210mm x 250mm

Completion
2015

Publisher
Tataro

Written by Lenka Mikovcova and illustrated by Vêra Ema Tataro, *Night Night Baby Heart* is a rhyming lullaby intended to help children from three to five years old relax at bedtime. The book is inspired by the children's book *Good Night Moon* (written by M. Wise Brown and illustrated by C. Hurd) and not only describes what children might see around them, but also helps children become aware of sounds and feelings. Knowing that children are sometimes afraid of the dark, the illustrations are designed to bring comfort and joy.

Night night, my tender midnight bre

Night night, my soap's sweet sme

Trix Trax

Author
Fran Ortega

Design Agency
Délire Design Studio

Designer
Luis Vanegas

Assistant Art
Christian Ortega

Size
210mm x 260mm

Completion
2015

Publisher
UNO Editorial

In 'Trix Trax' (*Tris Tras*), a set of unique characters includes an antique clock, a radio, a typewriter, and a library and they discover a place that reveals many secrets. Délire Design Studio's artistic concept was to playfully arouse children's interest for craft, and the design process included drawing, photography, storyboarding, and producing and final editing.

The book itself includes a cut-out character and an animation of this character is in the lower right-hand corner of the book. The color palette is based on the visual trend of illustration and images with a vintage touch. The font used in the layout is from TheMix Font Family.

de museo. Su
no pueden es-
zás son las me-
s usted un reloj

TRIS
TRAS

- Bueno, doctora, pensarían de mí que estoy chalado.
- Ja,ja,ja,ja- la Doctora Sabina no pudo contener su risa. ¿A ti
que te importa lo que piensen los demás? ¿Quién va a llevar los
números?

Tris-tras se ruborizo un poco.

- Eso te haría ser un reloj muy especial... ¿no crees?
- Daría la campanada, ¿verdad? Jajajaja...- Se rio Tris-tras imagi-
nándose su rostro de números distintos.
- Qué bien Tris-tras que te llenes de valor para ser tú mismo.
Muy bien, ya está, ya tenemos el remedio para tu enfermedad.
¿Has visto que era la más mala de todas pero la de más fácil
solución?
- ¿Y cómo lo vamos a hacer?
- Te voy a recetar números al gusto tuyo. Te voy a enviar a un
amigo mío que es uno de los mejores relojeros del mundo para
que te los instale. Y lo más importante; va a saber ver en ti, al
igual que yo, lo que aún no has descubierto de ti mismo.

- ¡¡Que ilusión Doctora!! Me encuentro supercontento.
La Doctora escribió la dirección y la receta donde ponía "Números al gusto del cliente". Tris-tras leyó el papel y puso cara de no
enterarse...

- ¿Dónde se encuentra este lugar?
- En la Ciudad de los Objetos Perdidos o no Inventados. – Añadió
la doctora con una sonrisa.

28

Tanto a mí, como a Tris-tras, debió quedársenos una cara de
tontos al no saber de qué nos estaba hablando. Sabina rompió
a reír, cogió un libro de magia de uno de sus estantes y al abrirlo,
apareció de entre sus páginas un arcoiris de relucientes colores.

- Es un libro mágico. El arcoiris que veis es un portal a la Ciudad
de Los Objetos Perdidos o no Inventados. Estas páginas os trans-
portarán a un lugar donde sólo los libros os pueden llevar.

Tris-tras y yo no podiamos creer lo que estábamos viendo.

29

Romania, What's That?

Designer
Mihaela Ana Comsa

Size
250mm x 250mm

Completion
2012

Publisher
**London College
of Communications,
University of
the Arts London**

This project contains a set of four interactive books that invite older children to learn about the cultural heritage, lifestyle, and natural scenery of Romania in a playful and graphic manner. All information is hidden within the visual work and revealed through die cutting and perforating, screen printing with photochromic ink, and the use of a reversible ink that can only be seen under sun or ultraviolet light.

Romania is an EU country, located in the Eastern Europe, with a territory of over
square miles

Positioned exactly half way between North Pole and Equator, Romania has a temperate-continental climate, with nice-hot summers...

...and snowy winters, perfect for skying and other winter sports.

About Lamb

Designer
Daria Maksimova

Size
170mm x 170mm

Completion
2012

'About Lamb' is a book for young children that tells the story of a lonely lamb travcling the world to find friends. The mixed-media illustrations are made using acrylic paint and newspaper collage. Daria Maksimova believes in a minimalist approach and that a story should be presented visually and understood easily, even without words. Thus, the designer's illustrations are intended to speak for themselves with no unnecessary elements or detail. The book has a simple red, blue, and yellow color palette, and text is included only as a supplement.

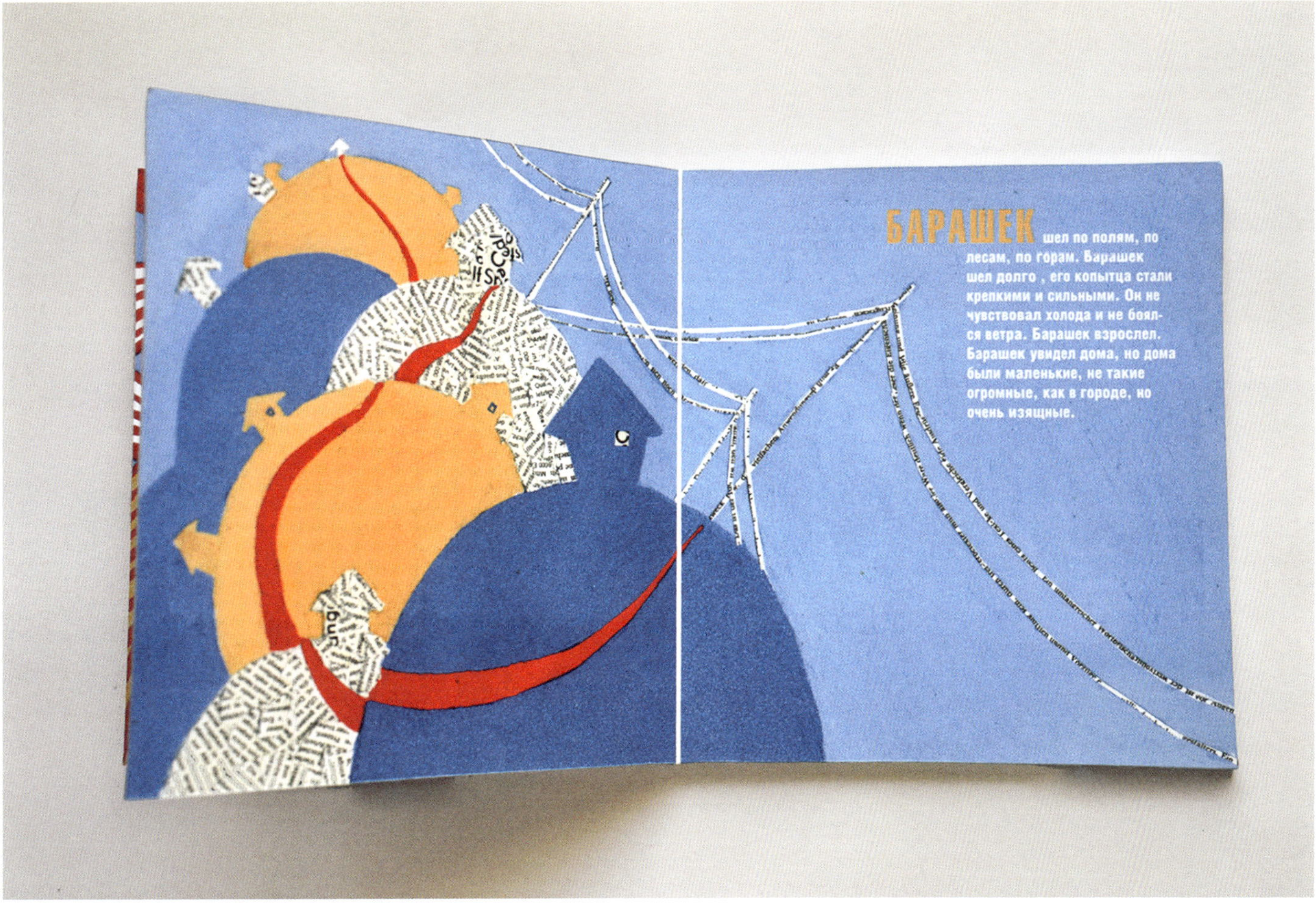

БАРАШЕК шел по полям, по лесам, по горам. Барашек шел долго , его копытца стали крепкими и сильными. Он не чувствовал холода и не боял-ся ветра. Барашек взрослел. Барашек увидел дома, но дома были маленькие, не такие огромные, как в городе, но очень изящные.

ОДНАЖДЫ ранним солнечным утром, груясь под лучами солнца, смотря на белоснежные кучерявые облака, барашек собрал-ся с духом, встал на свои маленькие, тоненькие нож-ки, поднял свой маленький хвостик и решил, что пора отправится на поиск друзей. Хватит всего бояться! Пора действовать!

Octopuses of a Same Tentacle Flock Together

Designer
Marcos Guardiola

Material
150gsm offset paper

Size
100mm x 100mm

Completion
2014

'Octopuses of a Same Tentacle Flock Together' (*Cada Pulpo Con Su Pulpa*) is a folded accordion book in which readers can discover odd pairs of connected animals that form a body that moves in a circular motion.

The designer aimed to develop an original, easy-to-produce format and tried different options of folding paper before using one double-sided sheet of paper (approximately 40cm by 40cm) cut to a spiral format. As children turn the book to read the story the animal body and texts run across each fold. The designer used only five colors and matched the backgrounds to each pair of animals.

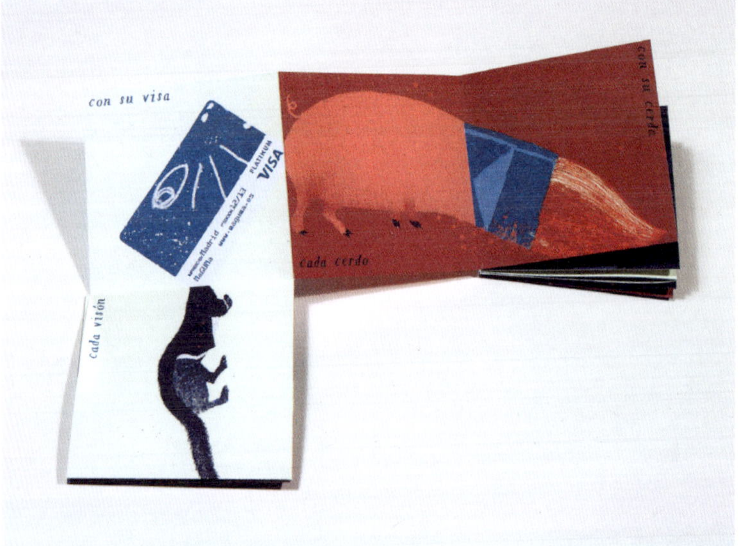

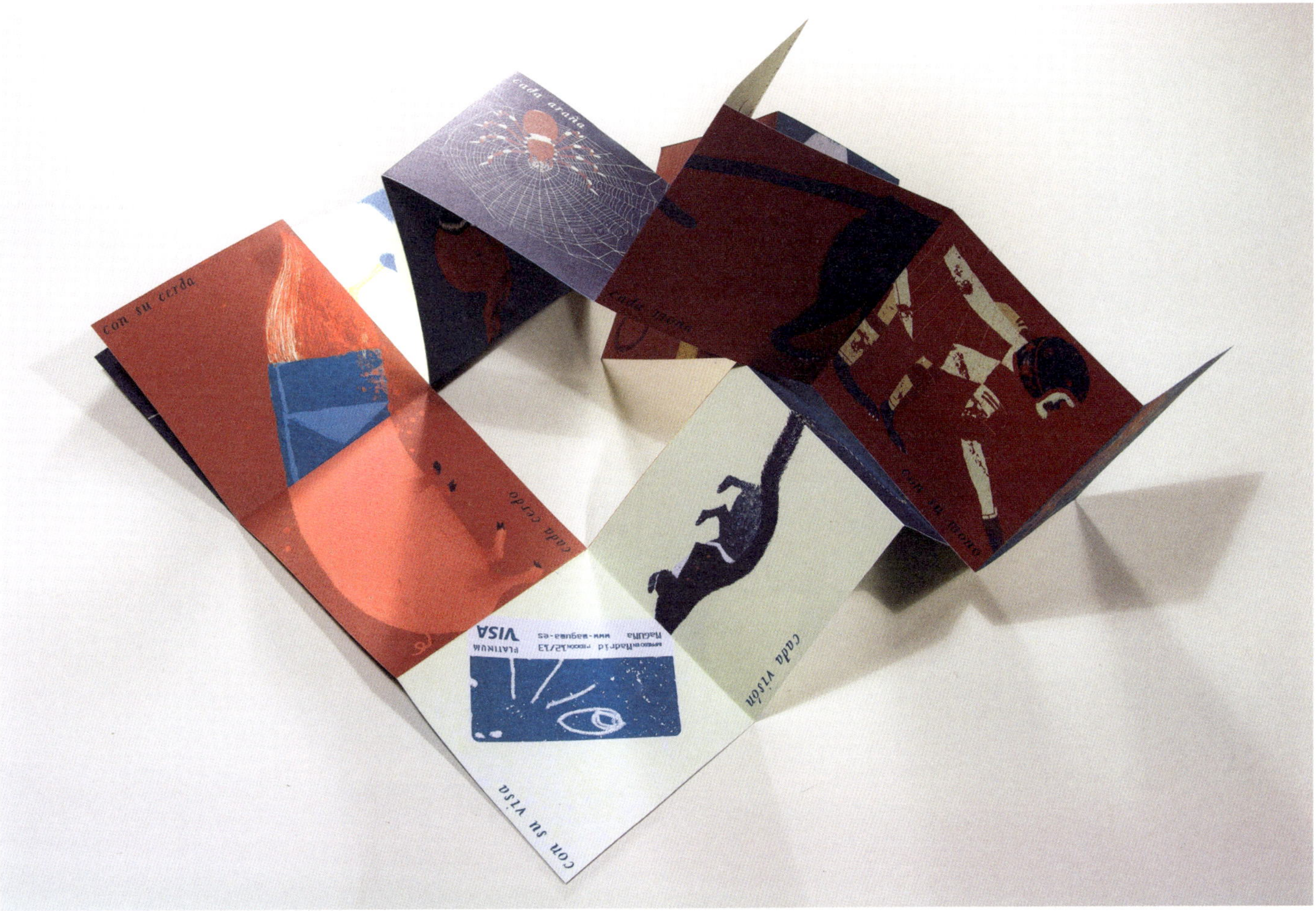

cada araña
con su cerda
cada cerdo
cada visón
con su visa

cada foca
cada burro
con su foco
con su flamenco
con su burra
cada ciga

Festina Lente Books

Designers
**Natalia Pérez Penagos,
Juliana Toro Suárez**

Material
Beige bond paper

Size
150mm x 150mm

Completion
2013

Publisher
Festina Lente Libros

Festina Lente is for older children and it comprises two books designed to physically embody the notion that, with books, readers can travel via their imagination. 'An Inventory of Words' (*El Inventariode Palabras*) is an A-to-Z encyclopedia presenting and documenting a series of magical creatures. Each entry has a freehand pointillist image and description with a piece of vellum paper containing handwritten messages. The binding enables the pages of the book to act as pockets that hold these messages and pink postcards. The postcards are a metaphor of how the book can transport readers to imaginary places and how the reader can travel the world via the book.

The second book, 'Eight Traveling Suns' (*8 Soles de Viaje*), is the anonymous diary of an explorer who traveled to fantastic imaginary places. The reader becomes part of the journey by writing the story and unfolding pages that mimic the narrative development. When the plot twists, so too does the book. In this way, reading the book becomes a physical experience as the reader is forced to turn the book in order to continue the story.

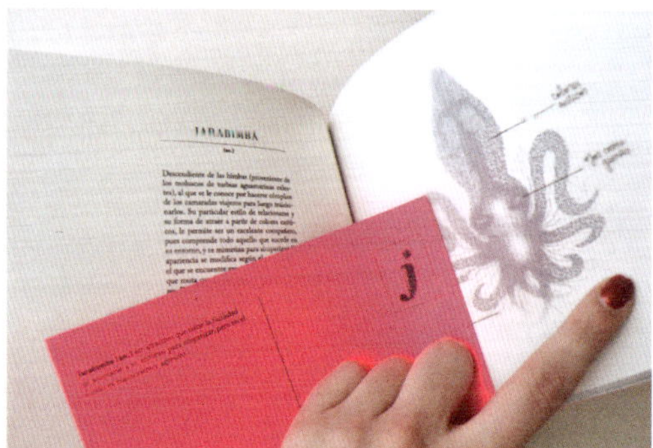

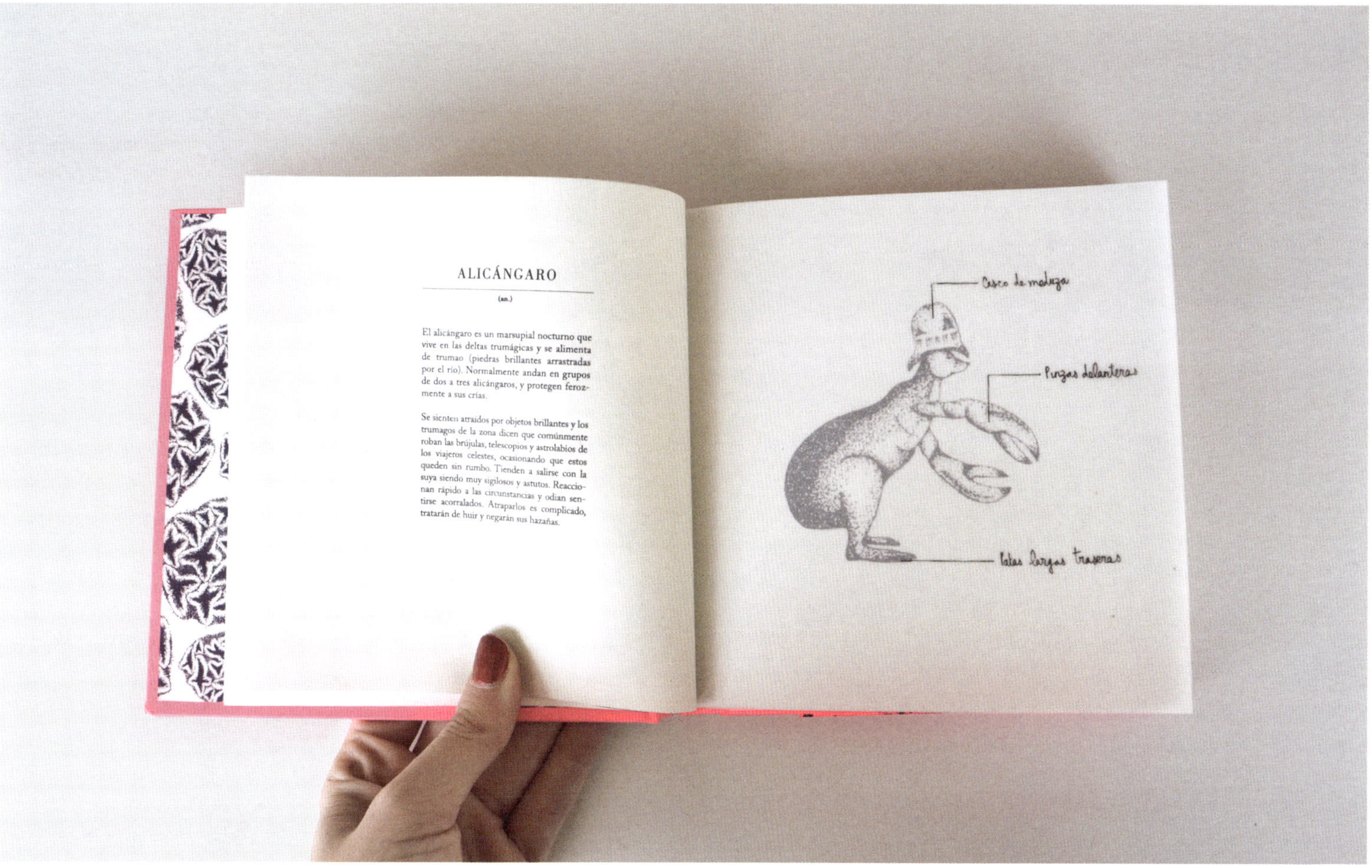

ALICÁNGARO

(sn.)

El alicángaro es un marsupial nocturno que vive en las deltas trumágicas y se alimenta de trumao (piedras brillantes arrastradas por el río). Normalmente andan en grupos de dos a tres alicángaros, y protegen ferozmente a sus crías.

Se sienten atraídos por objetos brillantes y los trumagos de la zona dicen que comúnmente roban las brújulas, telescopios y astrolabios de los viajeros celestes, ocasionando que estos queden sin rumbo. Tienden a salirse con la suya siendo muy sigilosos y astutos. Reaccionan rápido a las circunstancias y odian sentirse acorralados. Atraparlos es complicado, tratarán de huir y negarán sus hazañas.

Casco de medusa
Pinzas delanteras
Patas largas traseras

BAMBAZÚ

(dd.)

Nombre que se le otorga a la deidad que veneran las poblaciones aledañas al acantilado astrolunar de Mare Frigoris. Se atribuye a su ira la fuerza con la que el mar choca contra el acantilado, produciendo destellos de chispas color dorado marino. Aquellos que dicen haberlo visto lo identifican como una enorme nebulosa estelar que se alza del mar antes de grandes tormentas.

Los ritos que se practican en tributo a Bambazú se denominan bambuceos, que consisten en bailes frenéticos en los que la tribu ofrenda perlas boreales al dios durante cada solsticio lunar. Se dice que dicha ofrenda es el único regalo que calma su ira y apacigua las aguas durante tormentas.

chispas color dorado marino

Tyrannosaurus

Author
Tina Oziewicz

Designer
Ola Płocińska

Size
235mm x 235mm

Completion
2013

Publisher
Czerwony Konik

'Tyrannosaurus' (*Tyranozaur*) is a story of two girls that set off into the unknown and encounter a menacing Tyrannosaurus rex. Author Tina Oziewicz's story expresses sensitivity in seemingly ordinary things such as a carpet that hides a mysterious world.

Ola Płocińska integrated the illustrations and text throughout the entire spread. The designer used Calluna Sans font and created plants as illustrative elements. The chosen colors fit the mood of the story, which changes with the development of the plot.

Co to była za frajda! Przez wiele słonecznych dni dziewczynki podróżowały po tapecie z rysunkiem pól i łąk pełnych stokrotek i jagód, owocowych sadów i kolorowych uli. Na drzewach dojrzewały jabłka, gruszki i śliwki, w małych sadzawkach zarośniętych trzciną kumkały żaby, a powietrze buczało od pszczół. Gdy dojechały do framugi drzwi, były opalone i wypoczęte jak nigdy przedtem.

Niestety! Żaden talerz nie nadawał się na mieszkanie. Na jednym było napisane: SPAGHETTI, a kto by chciał mieszkać na spaghetti? Inny był cały w róże. Piękne, ale trzeba było patrzeć pod nogi, żeby się nie pokłuć o któryś z kolców, a gdyby traktor wjechał na jeden z nich, na pewno opona byłaby do wymiany. Na sąsiednim talerzu stał w dumnej pozie kogut. Gdy zobaczył nadjeżdżający traktor, wytrzeszczył oczy i najeżył się jak jeżozwierz (chociaż traktor był o wiele mniejszy od niego). Pozostałe talerze były w jasnoniebieską kratkę. Porce i Lana wjechały do jednego z nich i spróbowały się tam rozgościć, ale cały czas czuły się jak rybki w sieci.
Kiedy traktor objechał już wszystkie półki i dziewczynki obejrzały wszystkie talerze, westchnęły markotnie i postanowiły poszukać domu gdzie indziej. Wyjechały z szafki i ruszyły po ścianie kuchni, aż do sufitu. Gdyby ktoś, kto akurat jadł obiad przy stole, spojrzał wtedy w górę, zobaczyłby, jak malutki traktor przejeżdża powoli po suficie i znika w przedpokoju.

Inspector Blueberry and the Five Feathers of the Hoopoe

Designer
Karolina Benz

Size
245mm x 250mm

Completion
2013

'Inspector Blueberry and the Five Feathers of the Hoopoe' (*Kommissar Heidelbeer und die Fünf Federn des Wiedehopfs*) is designed for children aged five to seven years old and is based on the Sherlock Holmes cases. The cover title is hand lettered and the color-coordinated illustrations combine pictures and typography—named 'Benzinger' by the designer—to lead the reader's eyes over the page.

Fragen an Sie."
Wir kletterten den Baum hinunter und gingen zu ihrer Schlammpfütze.
„Ich hoffe für euch, es hat einen guten Grund, mich aus dem Schlaf zu reißen."
„Sie sind in Verdacht Herrn Wiedehopf entführt zu haben."
„Ihr habt wohl Salat im Kopf," gähnte sie.
„Wir haben eines ihrer Borstenhaare bei Herrn Wiedehopf im Nest gefunden, können Sie uns erklären wie es da hingekommen sein könnte?"
Sie schloss wieder ihre Augen. „Wen interessiert das?" gähnte sie.
„Kommissar Heidelbeer, Kommissar im Ruhestand und Rätsellöser von Beruf und meinen guten guten Freund Buchsel."
Mit diesen Worten glitt Kommissar Heidelbeer erleichtert neben Frau Wildschwein in die Schlammpfütze, vergrub sich bis zu seinen Augen in dem feuchten Dreck und verfeinerte sein Bad mit einer Prise Salz.
„Was tun Sie da mit meiner Schlammpfütze?"
„Ich bin ein Tintenfisch. Tintenfische brauchen Wasser, sonst trocknen sie aus und dann ist es vorbei mit ihnen."
„Na gut, wie war die Frage nochmal?" gähnte Frau Wildschwein.
„Wir haben eine Ihrer Borsten bei Herrn Wiedehopf im

In seinem vollen Federkleid stand Herr Wiedehopf vor uns.
„Was ist denn hier los, hat Frau Schuppentier jetzt endgültig jemand mit ihrem Tee umgebracht? Hehe!"
Bei der wiederholten Erwähnung von Frau Schuppentiers Tee begannen 92 Taumelkäfer und die 92 Wasserwanzen wieder unter meinem Panzer zu tanzen, und diesmal hatten sie alle ihre Familien dabei.
„Kommissar Heidelbeer, ich hab niemanden irgendwo hingetragen oder verschwinden lassen, ich wollte doch nur joggen gehen," kam Herr Honigdachs endlich zu Wort.
„Warum haben sie das nicht gleich gesagt, das ist ein wichtiger Hinweis."
„Aber Heidel, Herr Wiedehopf ist doch wieder da."
„Was ist denn hier los? hat Frau Schuppentier wirklich jemanden mit ihrem Tee vergiftet?"
„Ich kann es nicht bestätigen aber auch nicht widerlegen."
Mit diesen Worten ging er grübeln nach Hause. Nachdem ich mich zum Tee mit Herrn Wiedehopf für den nächsten Dienstag verabredet hatte, folgte ich meinem Mitbewohner.

Woody Loons

Designer
Agata Królak

Size
230mm x 320mm

Completion
2013

'Woody Loons' (*Gbury Tucholskie*) is a graphic novel for children and it features the trials and tribulations of a hypochondriac aristocrat in a rather unusual treatment facility.

Wanting to give the book a naïve look to clash with the strange and dream-like plot, Agata Królak used a handwritten typography to be concordant with the illustrations and to create an atmosphere of contradiction and oddity.

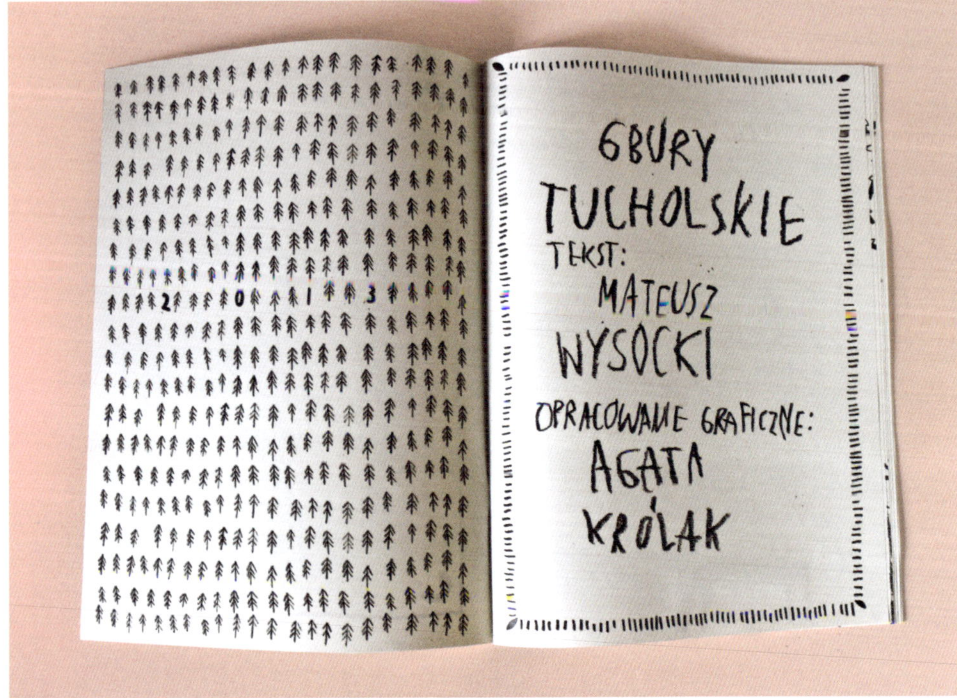

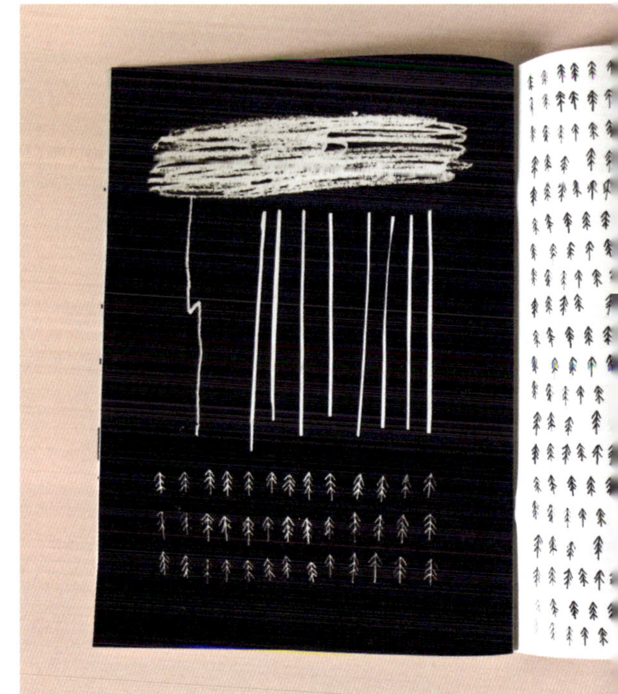

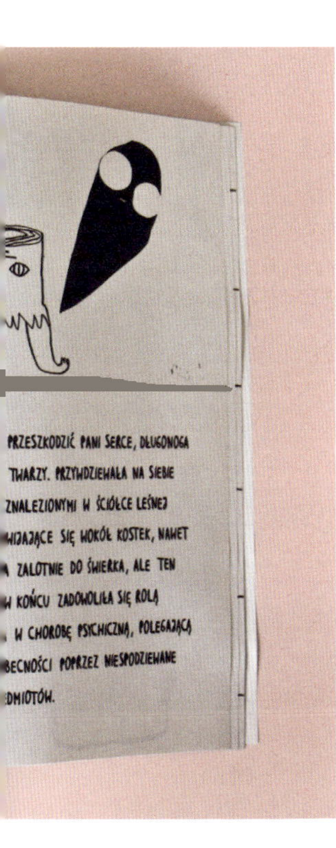

... PRZESZKODZIĆ PANI SERCE, DŁUGONOGA
... TWARZY. PRZYWDZIEWAŁA NA SIEBIE
... ZNALEZIONYMI W ŚCIÓŁCE LEŚNEJ
... ...WIJAJĄCE SIĘ WOKÓŁ KOSTEK, NAWET
... ...A ZALOTNIE DO ŚWIERKA, ALE TEN
... ...W KOŃCU ZADOWOLIŁA SIĘ ROLĄ
... W CHOROBĘ PSYCHICZNĄ, POLEGAJĄCĄ
... ...BECNOŚCI POPRZEZ NIESPODZIEWANE
... ...DMIOTÓW.

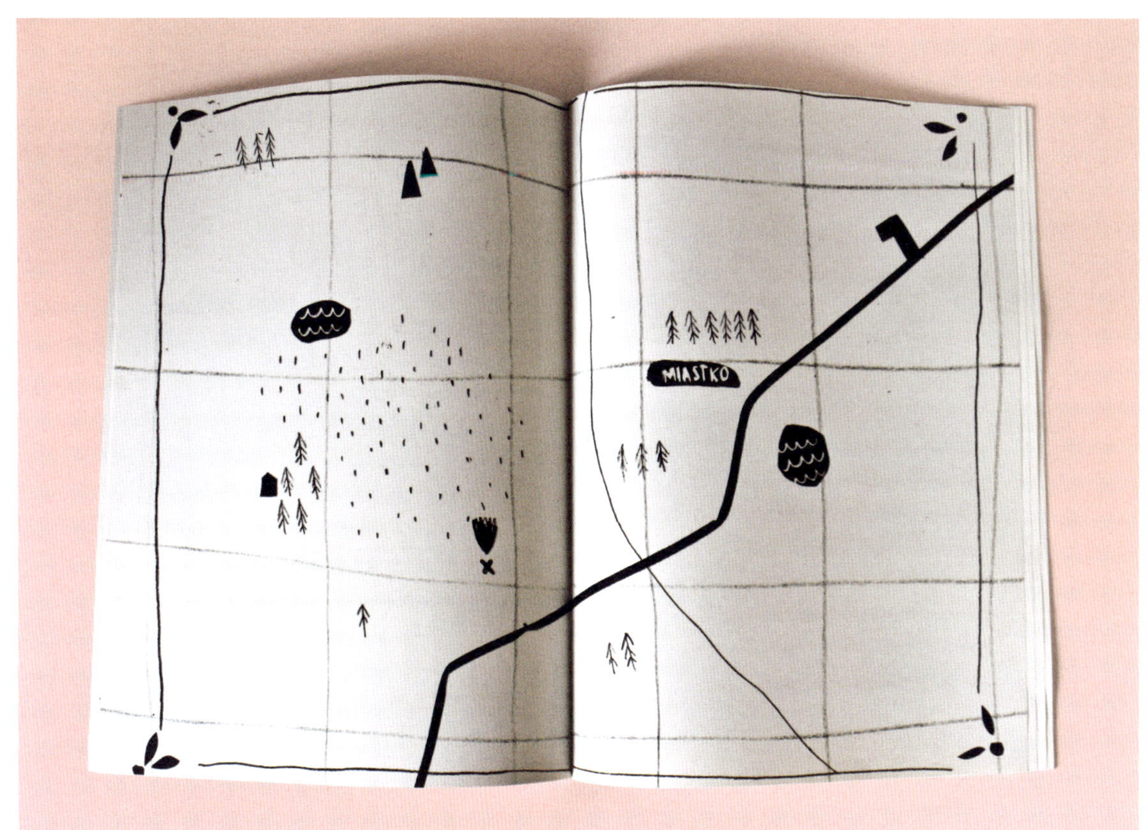

POZOSTAWIAJĄCĄ WIELE DO ŻYCZENIA CZTEROPIĘTROWĄ RUDERĘ ZAMIESZKIWAŁA BANDA PONURAKÓW O ZASTANAWIAJĄCYCH FIZJO-NOMIACH. PRZEZ DŁUGI CZAS NIE BYŁEM W STANIE ODRÓŻNIĆ PACJENTÓW OD LEKARZY. NIE NATKNĄŁEM SIĘ TAKŻE NA NIKO-GO ZE SŁUŻBY, MIMO REGULARNYCH UZUPEŁNIEŃ SŁOJÓW Z OGÓR-KAMI. KIEDY ZAPYTAŁEM O SOLIDNIEJSZĄ STRAWĘ WSKAZANO MI FORTEPIAN SPREPAROWANY ZASOLONYM MIĘSEM. POKÓJ NAPAWAŁ MNIE ODRAZĄ. POKRACZNE DESENIE NANIESIONE NA TAPETY POWODOWAŁY GĘSIĄ SKÓRKĘ I, GDYBY NIE MOJE DELIKATNE PALCE, Z PEWNOŚCIĄ ZERWAŁBYM JE ZE ŚCIAN.

Lullabies For All Family

Author
Anna Silivonchik

Designer
Olga Polesskova

Size
215mm x 224mm

Completion
2013

Publisher
Flavian

'Lullabies For All Family' features lyrics and drawings by well-known Belarusian artist Anna Silivonchik and includes a CD with lullabies performed by Natalia Faustova. Dreams and lullabies form one of Silivonchik's main subject matters.

Olga Polesskova used oil paint on canvas to create the illustrations and a whimsical font for the headings to foster a sense of miracle and fairy tale. The background of each spread is consistent throughout the book with darker edges and an illustration centered on one page of each spread. This is to suggest that the real world dissolves at night and dreams appear from the darkness.

Спи, мой ангел поднебесный

Музыка – А. Мисин, слова – С.Патрушев
Песня на диске 10

Спи, мой ангел поднебесный.
Спят деревья, спит вода.
От моей негромкой песни
Над тобой взойдёт звезда.

За далёкими холмами,
За соседнею стеной –
Сон с волшебными глазами
Ходит с лампою-луной.

Спи, мой ангел поднебесный.
Солнце за море зашло.
Всё, что будет – неизвестно.
Всё, что было – то прошло.

Всё приходит ниоткуда
И уходит в никуда.
Спи, малыш мой, спи, мой, будто.
Ты один здесь навсегда.

Спи, мой ангел поднебесный.
Ты ещё не знаешь зла.
Ты уже не слышишь песни.
Ты закрыл уже глаза.

За далёкими холмами
Старый сон тебя ведёт.
Дальше мне нельзя за вами.
Но кто же песню допоёт?

Колыбельная

Музыка – О.Фельцман, слова – Р.Гамзатов, Я.Козловский
Песня на диске 12

Какую песню спеть тебе, родная?
Спи. Ночь в июле только шесть часов.
Тебя, когда ты дремлешь, засыпая,
Я, словно колыбель, качать готов.

Спи. Ночь в июле только шесть часов.

Спокойной ночи! – говорю я снова
И верую, что не настанет дня,
Когда тебе два этих тихих слова
Промолвит кто-нибудь поздней меня.

Спи. Ночь в июле только шесть часов.

Пусть, милая, тебе спокойно спится.
А я пока долины осмотрю.
Скажу, чтоб вовремя запели птицы,
Задую звёзды и зажгу зарю.

Спи. Ночь в июле только шесть часов.

Banzai

Author
Zofia Fabjanowska-Micyk

Designer
Joanna Grochocka

Size
150mm x 235mm

Completion
2015

Publisher
Dwie Siostry Publishing House

Banzai is a children's guide to Japan with interesting stories about Japanese language, food, tea ceremony, origami, comics, Hello Kitty, and many other Japanese curiosities. Joanna Grochocka created colorful, vibrant illustrations to display the cultural and visual richness of Japan. The chapter title font is Kurokane Std EB; the body text font is Egyptian 505; and red text in the extra columns maintains a coherent color system.

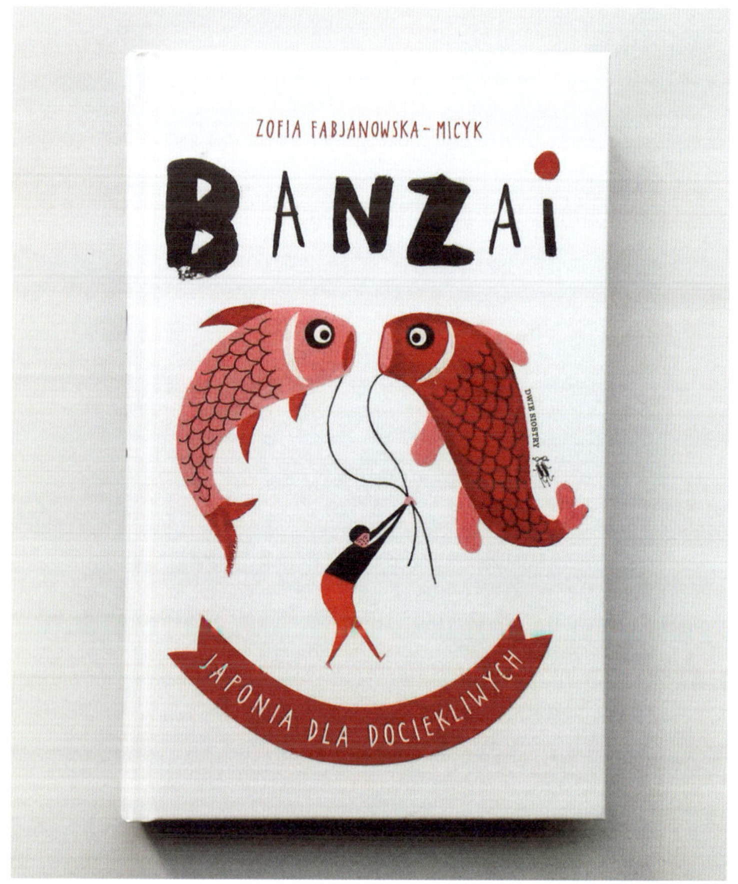

T jak kimono

66 Na początku XX wieku zaczęła się kariera jednego z najpopularniejszych ubrań w historii – T-shirtu. Trochę trwało, zanim prosta bawełniana koszulka w kształcie litery T się upowszechniła, ale dziś chętnie chodzi w niej dosłownie każdy – bez względu na wiek, płeć i styl. Tym bardziej że można ją kupić za grosze. Inne ubranie w kształcie litery T – starsze od T-shirtu o kilkaset lat – też stało się sławne, mimo że na pewno nie jest dla każdego. I nie da się o nim powiedzieć, że niewiele kosztuje. Mowa o **kimonie**, jednym z ważnych symboli Japonii.

„Kimono" znaczy dosłownie „rzecz do noszenia". Przed wiekami Japończycy określali tym słowem po prostu ubranie. Potem czasy się zmieniły i na Wyspy Japońskie dotarła moda z Europy i Ameryki: surduty, spodnie, koszule, suknie, kapelusze. A „kimono" stało się nazwą tradycyjnego japońskiego stroju.

Podobno wszystko zaczęło się pięć tysięcy lat temu w Chinach. Legenda głosi, że chiński cesarz lubił pić gotowaną wodę. Pewnego dnia zawiał wiatr i do jego kociołka z wrzątkiem wpadło kilka listków. Zabarwiły one wodę na złoto i nadały jej przyjemny aromat. Napój okazał się bardzo orzeźwiający. Była to pierwsza **herbata**.

Do Japonii herbata trafiła prawie cztery wieki później, a jej parzenie stało się w Kraju Kwitnącej Wiśni sztuką tak samo ważną jak układanie wierszy czy komponowanie muzyki.

Japończycy piją głównie zieloną herbatę. Smakuje inaczej niż czarna, którą u nas pije się na przykład z cukrem i cytryną. Co ciekawe, czarna herbata powstała podobno przez przypadek. Podczas transportu z Indii do Anglii zielone listki pociemniały i zaczęły inaczej pachnieć. Mimo to kupcy postanowili je sprzedać, nie chcieli stracić pieniędzy. Anglicy nie tylko nie zorientowali się, że coś jest nie w porządku, ale jeszcze polubili ten nowy smak.

Małe jest piękne 盆栽

92 Dziś właściwie wszystko ma wersję kieszonkową, mini czy mikro. Ale to wcale nie znaczy, że moda na pomniejszanie jest wynalazkiem naszych czasów. Japonia słynie z **bonsai**, czyli **miniaturowych drzew**. Najstarsze okazy liczą około 1000 lat. Słynną tysiącletnią minisosnę można oglądać w **Shunkaen**, parku-muzeum bonsai w Tokio. Malutkie drzewa nie są żadną specjalną odmianą normalnych drzew, nie da się kupić nasion, z których można je wyhodować. Jak zatem stworzyć taką miniaturkę? Podpowiedź kryje się w nazwie: po japońsku **bon** oznacza „płaską donicę" (**sai** to po prostu „roślina").

Wyobraźcie sobie młode drzewko, które rośnie w trudnych warunkach, na przykład nad urwiskiem albo w wąskiej szczelinie między skałami. Rozwija się na tyle, na ile starcza mu siły i miejsca. Korzeniami oplata kamienie, wygina się i przybiera fantastyczne

I Don't Want to Be a Princess

Author
Grzegorz Kadsepke

Designer
Agnieszka Matulka

Illustrator
Emilia Dziubak

Size
240mm x 320mm

Completion
2015

Publisher
**Armando
Curcio Editore**

The designers used Photoshop and a Wacom tablet to create 'I Don't Want to Be a Princess,' which tells the story of a girl who breaks down a stereotype. The book presents the main characters as a typical family living in an ordinary house in which the events that take place are familiar to children. The characters and their emotions are the most important elements of the story and the designers used sober colors—in contrast to what girls might typically like—and a light and transparent layout to make the book lighthearted and humorous.

Babcia oświadczyła, że nigdy, ale to nigdy nie uwierzy, że jej wnuczka może być aż tak straszliwym smokiem!

– Nawet jeżeli będę ziała ogniem? – zapytała Marysia. – A potem nie zjem deseru?!

– O, nie, to straszne... – wymamrotała babcia. – Jak można nie zjeść deseru?!

Tylko jeden jedyny dziadek uwierzył, że jego wnuczka może być aż tak straszliwym smokiem.

– Nie jesteś zdziwiony? – zdziwiła się Marysia.

– Ani trochę!

– I przeczuwałeś, że jest we mnie coś ze straszliwego smoka?

– Od dawna – pochwalił się dziadek. – Od chwili, gdy po raz pierwszy musiałem zmienić ci pieluchę!

Straszliwe smoki bawią się inaczej niz małe dziewczynki, ale jak – tego Marysia nie wiedziała.

– Pobaw się w teatr – zaproponował tata. – Ja będę...

– Rycerzem w zbroi! – zawołała Marysia.

– A mama...

– Księżniczką uwięzioną przez smoka! – oświadczyła Marysia.

– A ty?

– A ja będę sobą! – prychnęła Marysia. – Czyli tym smokiem właśnie.

– A my? – chciała wiedzieć babcia. – Kim będziemy ja i dziadek?

– Kościotrupami – wymyśliła Marysia. – Już dawno was zjadłam, wyplułam kosteczki i teraz leżycie nieruchomo na dywanie.

– Świetny pomysł! – zachwycił się dziadek

– Chyba żartujesz?! – wycedziła babcia.

– Ależ skąd! – oburszył się dziadek. – Uwielbiam leżeć nieruchomo na dywanie!

Little Secrets

Designer
Svetlana Minkova

Size
220mm x 165mm

Completion
2014

Photo Credit
Viktor Vinogradov

Publisher
Samokat Publishing House

Words play an active part in the illustrations of this lively book. Letters stand in lines, fly apart, compose a face, and pretend to be tree stems or kite tails. Letters also walk into a forest, fall like rain, and become tealeaves in a teacup. The book draws on a game in which children collect tiny objects and display them under a piece of glass like a magical window. Maria Kogon handcrafted the paper sculptures and paper images.

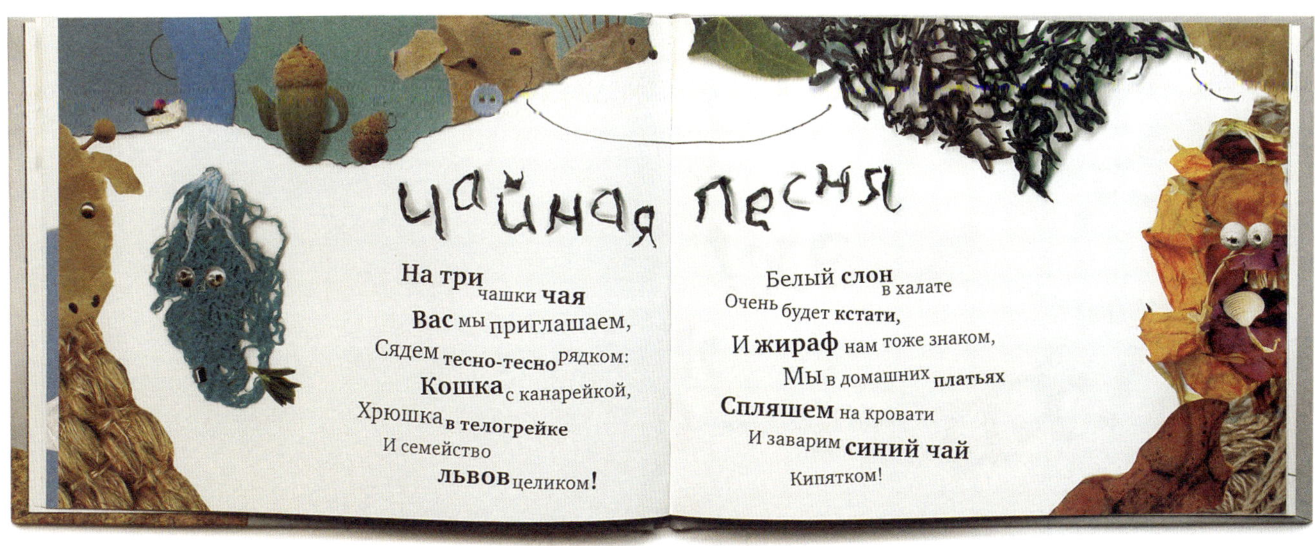

УДК 821.161.1-93
ББК 84-2(Рос=Русс)
М61

Минкова Светлана.
Секретики (для детей дошк. и мл. шк. возраста) /
Светлана Минкова. — М. Самокат, 2014. — 32 с. —
ISBN 978-5-91759-252-7

Сборник стихотворений. Секретики

© Минкова С.В, текст иллюстрации, макет, 2013
www.azbuku.ru

Литературно-художественное издание
Для детей дошкольного
и младшего школьного возраста

В соответствии с Федеральным законом № 436
от 29 декабря 2010 года «маркируется знаком 0+»

Иллюстрации: Светлана Минкова
Макет: Светлана Минкова
Корректор: Надежда Власенко
Директор издательства: Ирина Балахонова

В макете использована
бумага ручного литья Мэри Когон

Регистрационное свидетельство
№ 002.72.021 от 21.12.2001
ООО «Издательский дом «Самокат»
101000 Москва, а/я 487
+ 7 495 506 17 38
info@samokatbook.ru
www.samokatbook.ru

Подписано в печать 05.11.2013
Формат издания 90х70\16
Печать офсетная
Усл.печ.л. 3,51. Тираж 3000 экз.
Заказ № 5406/13

Отпечатано в соответствии
с предоставленными материалами
в ООО «ИПК Парето-Принт», г. Тверь
www.pareto-print.ru

The Alphabet
With Holes

Designer
Svetlana Minkova

Size
205mm x 215mm

Completion
2012

Photo Credit
Viktor Vinogradov

Publisher
Zhuk

Svetlana Minkova used collage and illustration to create the letters of the alphabet. Rhyming tongue twisters are intended to help readers remember vowels and consonants, and the 'holes' of the letters are designed to engage readers' imagination. For example, the hole in the letter Д is a kite on the other side of the page. The last spreads are designed for children and parents to work together to transform letters into images using crayons, colored papers, and soft-tip pens. The paper-made images are handcrafted by Maria Kogon, and the project was made with the support of Sorkin Studio.

Й
Йод
Ой! Ой! Ой!
Ай! Ай! Ай!
Лучше йод
Не проливай!
йод

«П» – прихожая, понятно,
Там нам прятаться приятно!

Ш
Шапка
«Ш» – это шапка у нашего Сашки,
Уши у шапки, как у Степашки!

World Wide Fairy Tales in Poems

Design Agency
Lá Studio

Illustrators
**Nguyen Thanh Vu,
Pham Hoang Giang**

Size
250mm x 250mm

Completion
2014

Publisher
Kim Đồng Publishing House

'World Wide Fairy Tales in Poems' relays eight common stories as funny and memorable poems. To counter the challenge of these traditional stories being well known to children, Lá Studio created new images of the characters and their worlds by giving them totally different appearances and characteristics and matching the illustrations to the modern poems.

Most stories are told in four or five spreads with more than two scenes on one spread. The designers used a flat and simple style to compose and connect these scenes.

Thế mà rồi sau đó,
Vì công chuyện, đi xa
Vì nhiều chuyện khác nữa,
Nên khi quay về nhà

Ông mới nhớ đến nó.
Cô bé nghèo bán diêm
Co ro trong góc phố,
Thu mình giữa bóng đêm.

Ông nháo nhào tìm kiếm,
Chiếc áo lông trên tay.
Và khóc khi biết nó,
Chết trước đấy mấy ngày.

Vẫn bên góc phố ấy,
Ông ngồi, khóc trong đêm.
"Bác ơi, cháu xin bác
Mua giùm cháu bao diêm..."

Cả thành phố rực rỡ
Vì đang là Nô-en.
Ông thấy nó đứng đó,
Co ro dưới cột đèn.

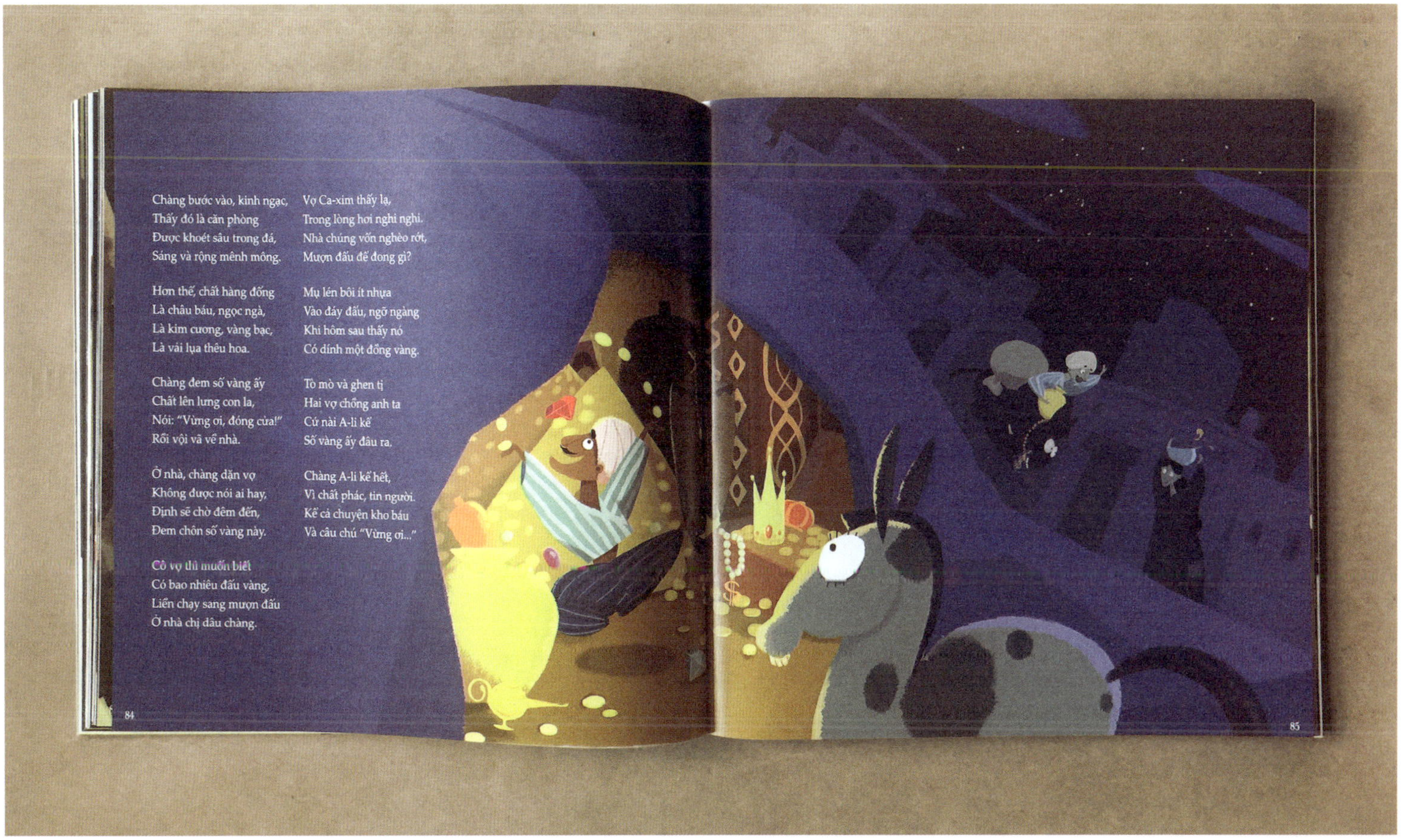

Chàng bước vào, kinh ngạc,
Thấy đó là căn phòng
Được khoét sâu trong đá,
Sáng và rộng mênh mông.

Hơn thế, chất hàng đống
Là châu báu, ngọc ngà,
Là kim cương, vàng bạc,
Là vải lụa thêu hoa.

Chàng đem số vàng ấy
Chất lên lưng con la,
Nói: "Vừng ơi, đóng cửa!"
Rồi vội vã về nhà.

Ở nhà, chàng dặn vợ
Không được nói ai hay,
Định sẽ chờ đêm đến,
Đem chôn số vàng này.

Cô vợ thì muốn biết
Có bao nhiêu đấu vàng,
Liền chạy sang mượn đấu
Ở nhà chị dâu chàng.

Vợ Ca-xim thấy lạ,
Trong lòng hơi nghi nghi.
Nhà chúng vốn nghèo rớt,
Mượn đấu để đong gì?

Mụ lén bôi ít nhựa
Vào đáy đấu, ngỡ ngàng
Khi hôm sau thấy nó
Có dính một đồng vàng.

Tò mò và ghen tị
Hai vợ chồng anh ta
Cứ nài A-li kể
Số vàng ấy đâu ra.

Chàng A-li kể hết,
Vì chất phác, tin người.
Kể cả chuyện kho báu
Và câu chú "Vừng ơi..."

Rất sâu dưới đáy biển,
Giữa mịt mù xa khơi,
Có một thế giới đẹp,
Đẹp lung linh, tuyệt vời.

Các nàng tiên cá hát
Những bài ca du dương,
Hay đến mức thủy thủ,
Để tàu đi lạc đường.

Vua Thủy Tề oai vệ
Sống trong cung của ngài,
Chỉ suốt ngày yến tiệc,
Rất hiếm khi ra ngoài.

Từ ngày vợ vua chết,
Mọi việc trong triều đình
Đều do thái hậu quản,
Hợp lí và thông minh.

Bà là người quyền lực,
Tốt bụng nhưng kiêu sa.
Ai bà cũng yêu quý,
Nhất là các cháu bà.

Cháu bà, toàn cháu gái,
Năm nàng, đẹp như tiên,
Tất cả đều nhí nhảnh,
Vui tươi và dịu hiền.

Mụ nghe gương nói thế
Liền tái mặt vì ghen
Một hôm bèn cho gọi
Ông lão thợ săn già:

"Ngươi phải đem Bạch Tuyết
Vào sâu trong rừng dày,
Giết chết và sau đấy
Mang gan nó về đây!"

Vốn thương người, ông lão
Không đang tâm giết nàng
Để lừa mụ hoàng hậu,
Ông giết một con mang.

Lại nói nàng Bạch Tuyết,
Một mình giữa rừng cây,
Nàng sợ, nhưng không biết
Phải làm gì lúc này.

Nàng cứ đi đi mãi,
Cho đến khi bất ngờ
Thấy một ngôi nhà lá
Bé nhỏ và đơn sơ.

Đi nhiều nên đói, mệt.
Mà cũng đã tối trời,
Nàng quyết định dừng lại,
Xin vào nhà nghỉ ngơi.

Người ta kể, lần nọ
Vào một tối mùa đông,
Ở thủ đô Đan Mạch,
Trời thấp, nhiều sương mù,

Có một người mảnh khảnh,
Đầu đội mũ cao vành
Đang thong thả đi dạo
Dọc bờ sông yên lành,

Một tay cầm cuốn sách,
Tay kia giơ lên trời,
Bắt những bông tuyết nhỏ,
Tuyết đầu mùa, đang rơi.

Bỗng có giọng lí nhí
Vang lạnh giữa trời đêm:
"Bác ơi, cháu xin bác
Mua giùm cháu bao diêm!"

Đó là một bé gái
Tuổi khoảng chín hay mười.
Áo rách, run vì lạnh,
Túi diêm đeo bên người.

52

Và nếu chàng hoàng tử
Không thực sự yêu ngươi
Như con yêu bố mẹ,
Ngươi sẽ không thành người.

Nếu chàng cưới người khác
Thì rạng sáng hôm sau,
Ngươi chết, thành bọt biển
Trôi giữa sóng bạc đầu..."

Nàng tiên cá chấp nhận
Tất cả những điều này.
Ôi, tâm hồn bất tử,
Ôi, tình yêu mê say.

Đối lại, mụ phù thủy
Đòi giọng hát của nàng,
Một giọng hát kì diệu,
Du dương và dịu dàng.

Tay cầm lọ thuốc độc,
Nàng tiên cá dịu hiền
Bơi một vòng từ biệt
Rồi nhẹ nhàng lao lên.

Mặt trời còn chưa mọc,
Chàng hoàng tử của nàng
Đang trầm ngâm ngắm biển,
Tay tì lên cầu thang.

Nàng uống hết lọ thuốc,
Thấy cháy cổ, và rồi
Như có lưỡi kiếm sắc
Xé thân nàng làm đôi.

112

About Bunnies

Design Agency
Angelina Slatina

Material
300gsm coated litho paper

Size
200mm x 200mm

Completion
2014

Publisher
Zebra Printing House

'About Bunnies' (*Pro Kro*) is a book for children at nursery school and kindergarten. It is a story about the life of a bunny and each page tells a new story with short verses about different events and situations, such as how bunnies—like people—have friends, travel, and fall in love.

The watercolor illustrations are sensitive, soft, and detailed enough that children can examine the bunny's house and environment. A fun game for children is to find a little mouse that hides in almost every illustration. The text is on the reverse side of each image and the pages are decorated with painted elements.

Софи хотела стать принцессой,
Самой настоящей.
Она ходила в пышном платье,
А жить хотела в башне.

И в комнате поставив трон,
Приказы отдавала,
А делать добрые дела,
Принцесса забывала!

27

В лесу на полянке
Растет земляника,
Ее собирают
Крольчата с крольчихой.

А вечером дома
Сварят варенье,
И будет для всех
На столе угощенье.

43

Don't Like It—
Don't Listen

Designer
Rita Cherepanova

Material
100gsm recycled paper,
soft cover

Size
190mm x 140mm

Completion
2015

'Don't Like It—Don't Listen' is based on several fairy tales written by Stepan Pisakhov and it tells the story of a teenage girl that goes to the Russian village of Uima during the summer holidays and an elderly man tells her fantastic stories that become reality.

Rita Cherepanova looked at Russian folktales through the eyes of a modern city girl to demonstrate how folk art can be fresh and interesting and worth a closer look. The result is a book that mixes a graphic novel with a traditional tale. The designer used the Pragmatica typeface for the story text and handmade lettering for the titles and page numbers to visually connect the text with the illustrations. 'Real world' illustrations are in black gouache and 'fairy tale' illustrations in cyan, pink, and yellow, with extra details added in Photoshop.

"

ПЛЯШЕТ САМОВАР
ПЛЯШЕТ ПЕЧКА

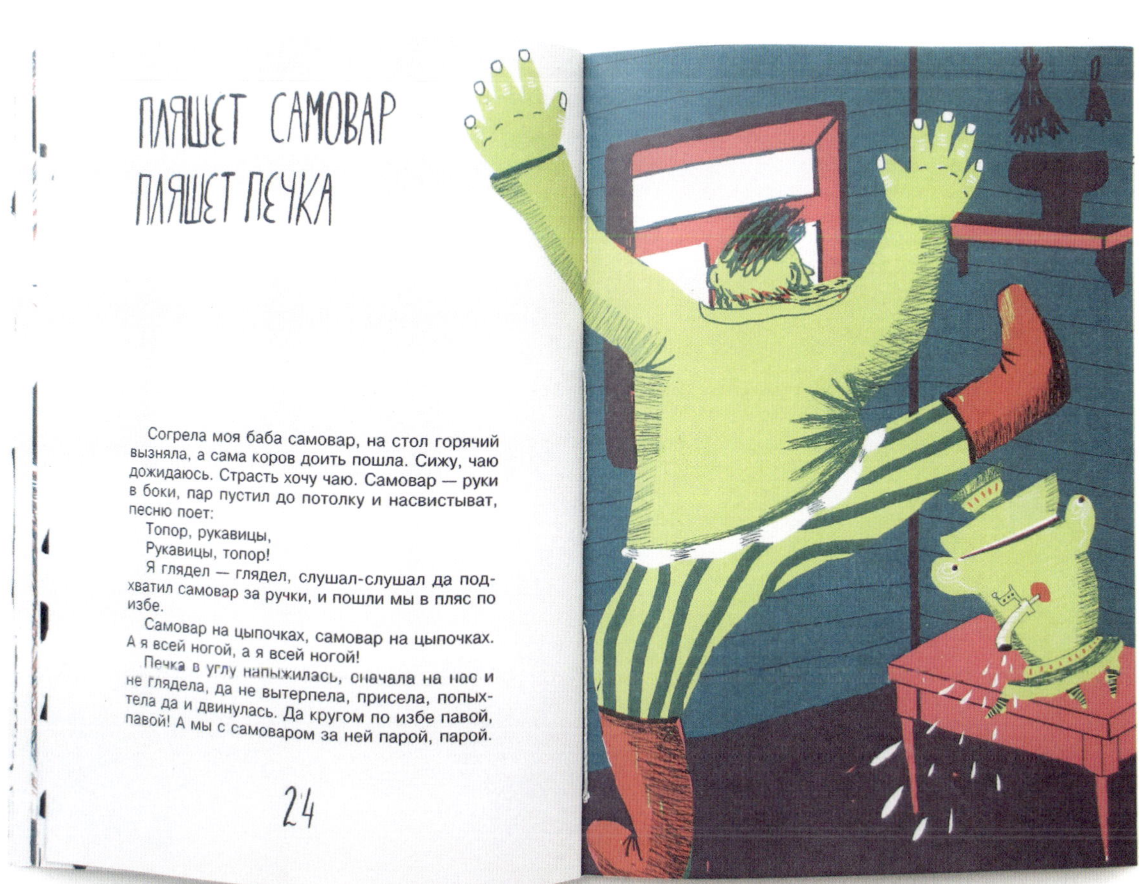

Согрела моя баба самовар, на стол горячий вызняла, а сама коров доить пошла. Сижу, чаю дожидаюсь. Страсть хочу чаю. Самовар — руки в боки, пар пустил до потолку и насвистыват, песню поет:

Топор, рукавицы,
Рукавицы, топор!

Я глядел — глядел, слушал-слушал да подхватил самовар за ручки, и пошли мы в пляс по избе.

Самовар на цыпочках, самовар на цыпочках. А я всей ногой, а я всей ногой!

Печка в углу напыжилась, сначала на нас и не глядела, да не вытерпела, присела, попыхтела да и двинулась. Да кругом по избе павой, павой! А мы с самоваром за ней парой, парой.

24

Налим в окошечко выскользнул — и ко мне. Я опять к протопопу. Протопоп обрадел и говорит:

— Как бы ишшо таку налимину, дак как раз в мой аппетит будет!

Опять рупь дал, опять протопопиха в кладовку вынесла налима. Налим тем же ходом в окошечко, да и опять ко мне.

Взял я налима на цепочку и повел, как собаку. Налим хвостом отталкиватся, припрыгиват-бежит.

На трамвай не пустили. Кондукторша требовала бумагу с печатью, что налим не рыба, а есть собака охотничья.

Ну, мы и пешком до дому доставились.

Дома в собачью конуру я поставил стару квашню с водой и налима туда пустил. На калитку записку налепил: «Остерегайтесь цепного налима». Чаю напился, сел к окну покрасоваться, личико рученькой подпер и придумал нового сторожа звать Налим Малиныч.

не закатыватся: ему на одном месте стоять скучно, ну, оно и крутит по небу. В сутки раз пятьдесят обернётся, а коли погода хороша да поветерь, то и семьдесят; коли дождь да мокреть, так солнце отдыхат, стоит.

А на том берегу всяка благодать, всяческо благорастворение. Морошка крупна, ягоды по три фунта и боле, и всяка друга ягода.

Семга да тресда сами ловятся, сами потрошатся, сами солятся, сами в бочки ложатся. Рыбаки только бочки порозны к берегу подкатывают да днища заколачивают. А котора рыба побойче — выпотрошится да в пирог завернется. Семга да палтусина ловче всех рыб в пирог заворачиваются. Хозяйки только маслом смазывают да в печку подсаживают.

Белы медведи молоком торгуют — приучены. Белы медвежата семечками и папиросами промышляют. Птички всяки чирикают: полярны совы, чайки, гаги, гагарки, гуси, лебеди, северны орлы, пингвины.

Пингвины у нас хоть не водятся, но приезжают на заработки, с шарманкой ходят да с бубном, а ины облизьяной одеваются, всяки штуки представляют, им в не пристало облизьяной одеваться — ноги коротки, ну, да мы не привередливы, нам хоть и не всамделишна облизьяна, лишь бы смешно было.

А в большой праздник да возьмутся пингвины с белыми медведями хороводы водить, да еще

вприсядку пустятся, ну, до уморенья! А моржи да тюлени с нерпами у берега в воде хлюпают да поуркивают — музыку делают по-своему.

А робята поймают кита или двух, привяжут к берегу и заставят для прохлаждения воздуха воду столбом пускать. А бурым медведям ход настрого запрещен. По-зажилыо столбы понаставлены и над-писи на них: «Бурым медведям ходу нет».

Раз вез мужик муки мешок. Это было вверху, выше Лявли. Вот мужик и обронил мешок в лесу. Медведь нашел, в муке вывалялся весь и стал на манер белого. Стащил лодку да приехал в город: его водой да поветерью несло, он рулем ворочал. До рынка доехал, на льдину пересел. Думал сначала промышлять семечками да квасом, а как разживется, и самогоном торговать. Да его узнали — как не узнать? — обличье-то показало! Что смеху было! В воде выкупали. Мокрехонек, фыркат, а его с хохотом да с песнями робята за город прогнали.

Медведь заплакал от обиды. Народ у нас добрый: дали ему вязку калачей с анисом, сахару полпуда да велели кой-когда за шаньгами приходить.

42

Pop-up
Books

Bobropediya

Design Agency
Great Advertising Group

Designers
Artem Kostyukevich,
Gennadiy Sukhov,
Andrey Mordovtsev

Material
Paper, cardboard

Printing Technology
Gloss varnish, matte laminate

Size
240mm x 240mm

Completion
2014

Bobropediya was designed for the children of BBR Bank's clients to increase brand loyalty and promote positive feelings toward the bank. The word 'beaver' is in consonance with 'BBR' and it became the basis of the story. Each of the pop-up book's nine spreads humorously retells a story from a classic book. Illustrations are accompanied by funny poems and texts with constructive solutions.

Вот Гадкий утёнок подходит к пруду,
Где цапли, танцуя, хватают еду,
Где гуси гудят в самодельные дудки
И шутят дрозды откровенные шутки.
Утёнок рыдает, в печали неистов.
Но мудрый бобёр подбодрил пессимиста:
«Ты гадким утёнком явился на бал,
Влюбился, женился и лебедем стал».

A Short Story About Time

Designer
Mariana Crespo Allen

Material
Paper, cardboard

Size
111mm x 297mm

Completion
2015

This pop-up book explains how people have read and interacted with time in different eras and different countries. The first spread is set in the morning in Ancient Egypt; the second is in London in the afternoon in the 1860s; and the third is at night in Tokyo in the 2000s.

Pop-ups are intended to stimulate young readers' interest and curiosity in the concept of time. Mariana Crespo Allen made the three-dimensional pop-ups from a single sheet of paper using the folding and cutting paper-art technique of kirigami. The illustrations combine limited color palettes and simple geometric shapes derived from children's building blocks. The elongated shape accommodates the tall pop-ups and it is intended to stand out and be fun for children to hold.

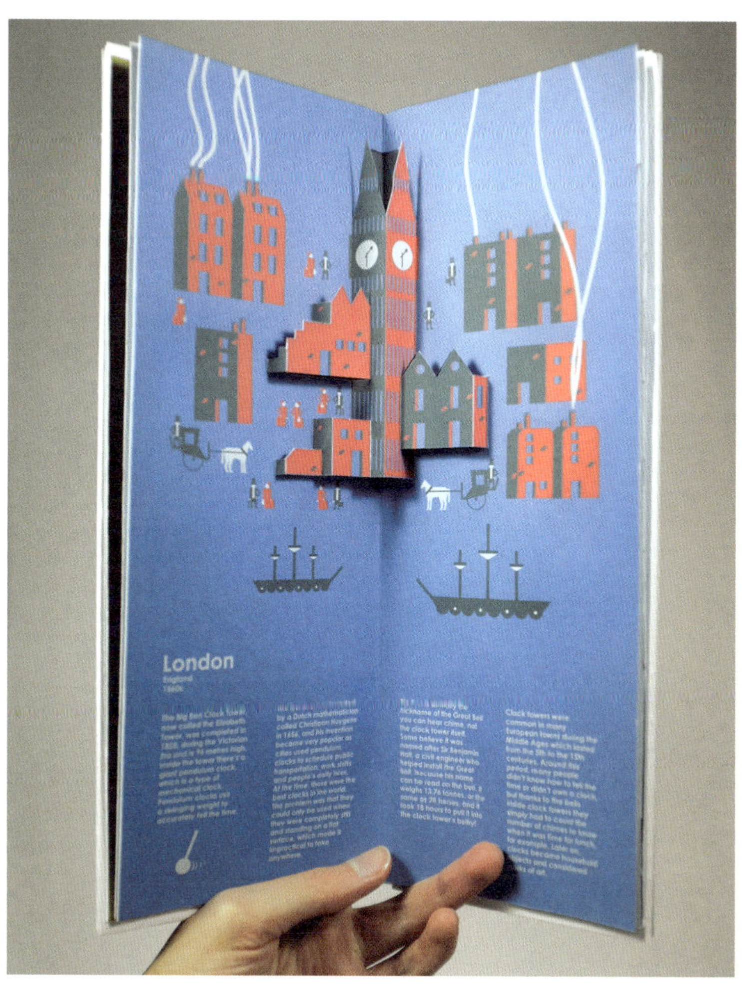
London
England
1859

Tokyo

Heliopolis
Egypt
c.1930 BC

Tokyo

The Lazy Puffy

Designer
Ubonwanna Klinjuy

Material
Paper, cardboard

Printing Technology
UV varnish, paper craft

Size
185mm x 260mm

Completion
2014

The Lazy Puffy is designed to encourage young students to read and it tells a fantasy story about the animals that happily live in 'The Puffy Forest.' The book is in English and Thai and the designer diligently cut every piece of paper—an intricate and time-consuming process—making it a handmade and heart-felt project. Learning materials include felt masks, paper puppets, and bookmarks.

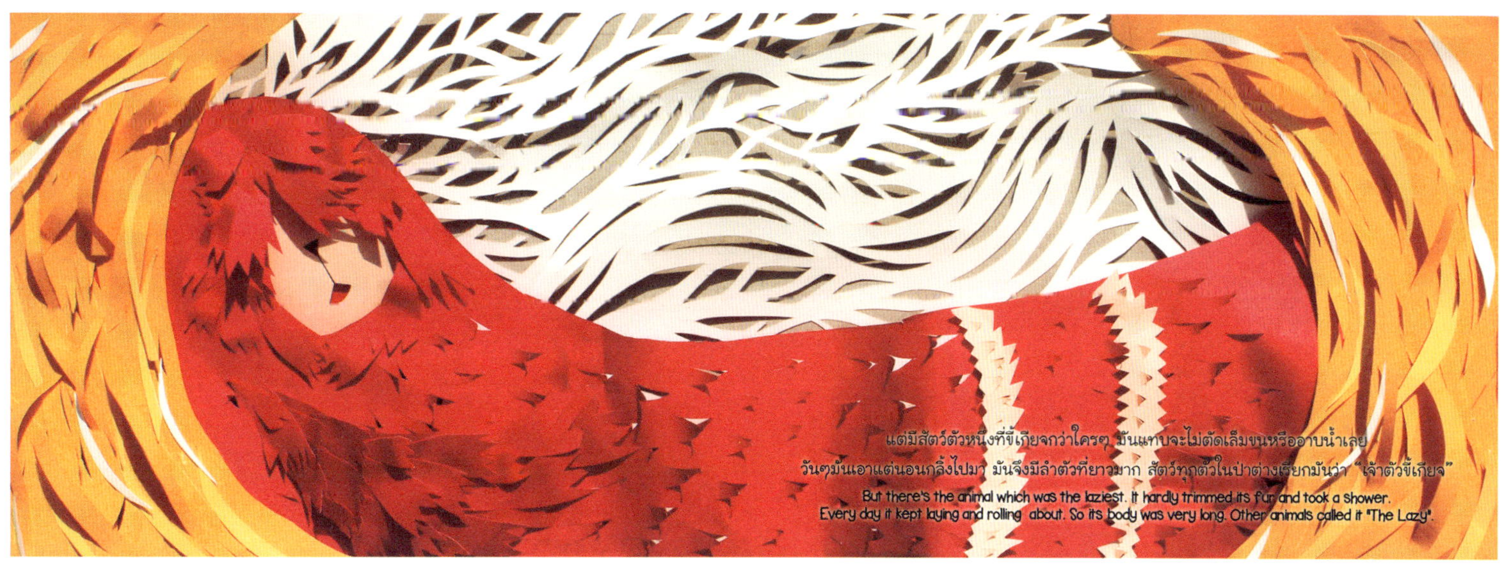

แต่มีสัตว์ตัวหนึ่งที่ขี้เกียจกว่าใครๆ มันแทบจะไม่ตัดเล็มขนหรืออาบน้ำเลย
วันๆมันเอาแต่นอนกลิ้งไปมา มันจึงมีลำตัวที่ยาวมาก สัตว์ทุกตัวในป่าต่างเรียกมันว่า "เจ้าตัวขี้เกียจ"
But there's the animal which was the laziest. It hardly trimmed its fur and took a shower.
Every day it kept laying and rolling about. So its body was very long. Other animals called it "The Lazy".

เจ้าสัตว์ประหลาดทั้งหลายชอบเข้ามาก่อกวนป่าปุกปุยอยู่เรื่อย สัตว์ในป่าปุกปุย
จึงต้องคอยแก้ปัญหากันอยู่เสมอ ทุกตัวจึงหวาดกลัวเจ้าสัตว์ประหลาดมาก
All monsters always liked to agitate the Puffy Forest. And the animals here had to solve
the problems. So they all were afraid of the monsters.

สัตว์ต่างๆจึงเตรียมอาวุธ เพื่อไปต่อสู้และขับไล่
เจ้าสัตว์ประหลาดให้ออกไปจากป่า
แล้วทุกตัวก็มุ่งหน้าไปตามเสียงร้องโหยหวนที่ได้ยิน
ทุกตัวเดินตามเสียงร้องมา จนในที่สุดก็มาถึงหน้าบ้านหลังหนึ่ง
"นี่มันบ้านของเจ้าตัวขี้เกียจนี่นา"
สัตว์ตัวหนึ่งพูดขึ้นแล้วเสียงร้องโหยหวนก็ดังขึ้นอีก
ทุกตัวจึงเตรียมบุกเข้าไปในบ้านของเจ้าตัวขี้เกียจ
They prepared weapons to fight and drive away
the monster out of the Puffy Forest.
Then they were heading to the weird groaning voice
Finally the voice led them to a house.
"This is The Lazy's house." One of the animals said.
Then the groaning came up again.
All animals got ready to break into The Lazy's house.

There Was Once a King

Designer
Dominika Godlewska

Material
Handmade paper, canvas,
acrylic paint, cardboard

Size
200mm x 150mm

Completion
2015

'There Was Once a King' (*Był Sobie Król*) is a tale from the stories collected by A. J. Gliński in *Polish Storyteller* printed in 1862. Dominika Godlewska's book is a combination of illustrations, texts, and pop-ups. It is made of handmade paper and linen with monotype and Gothic font for a medieval feel. The designer created a disquieting atmosphere in the illustrations to reflect the story becoming darker as it develops. Godlewska believes children need to know the reality of the world and that they like to be scared and do not need their hands held all the time.

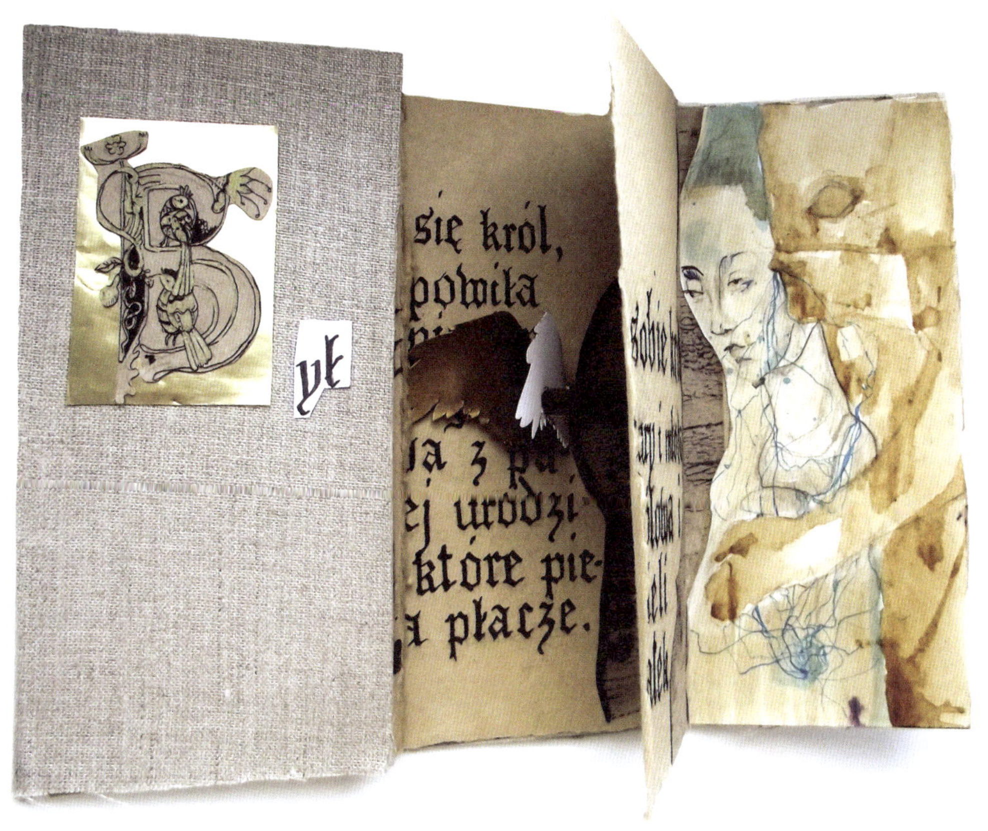
się król,
powiła
ą z pa
ej urodzi
które pie-
a płacze.
yk

Duszo świata;
słonko jasne
Zajrzyj w me więzienie
ciasne
Zlituj się nade
mną
Powiedz gdzie
ulubiony
Jakie teraz zwiedza
strony
Czy przybędzie do mnie

The Playful Dough

Designer
Linh Trinh

Size
148mm x 210mm

Completion
2012

The Playful Dough is an educational and informative book with a poignant feel and it features Tò he, a popular dough figurine toy in Vietnam and China. Linh Trinh's design invites readers to touch, flip, and explore the tactile book. The designer used V-fold and stand-up pop-up techniques as a medium of storytelling, and lengthy lists are translated into history wheels, flipbooks, and pull-up windows.

The vintage-washed color palette is sampled from 1990s textbooks in which images are silk-screened in blocks of bright, primary colors. Trinh created illustrations through a mix of pen sketches, watercolors, and pastels, as well as digital processing. The vibrant and playful pop-ups, and simple, clean graphic touches make this book suitable for children and adults with a childlike innocence.

STREET
ART
'CUL-
TURE

However, it still remains a myth for children
every kid had once tried a small, tasteless
bite just out of innocent curiosity. And it
goes on to be one of the best-loved memory
... as children of so many generations

Once Upon a Time

Designer
Yi-Chen Lin

Material
Art drawing paper,
halftone paper

Printing Technology
Embossing, debossing,
matte PP paper

Size
280mm x 280mm

Completion
2014

'Once Upon a Time' is designed to encourage children's interest in Taiwanese folk stories by integrating the tales with basic theory and traditional Chinese games. The format and typography is inspired by the games Snakes and Ladders, and Tangram. 'The Smeller' converts a two-dimensional route into three dimensions so players need to 'go up' to win. In 'Sun Moon Lake' players rearrange the game boards to make new routes.

妙鼻司
THE COOPERATIVE POP-UP GAME BOOK
PAPER ENGINEERING
& ILLUSTRATORS
BY
LIN YI-CHEN

Beyond the Walls

Designer
Adrian Panadero

Material
Card stock, sticker paper, chip board

Size
241mm x 267mm

Completion
2015

The aim of *Beyond the Walls* is to remind young readers of the significance of the Philippines' historic capital Intramuros and to encourage children's curiosity about its history and spark their passion to preserve it.

The designer used paper engineering so readers can open flaps, insets, and gate-folds to reveal maps, interior structures, and stories of historical events and figures. Similarly, the book's layout is complicit in achieving the goal of letting readers unravel Intramuros' story themselves. The texts are laid out in the foldable parts to build the city's story step by step and vivid colors are designed to bring the history topic to life. A legible slab serif typeface improves ease of reading.

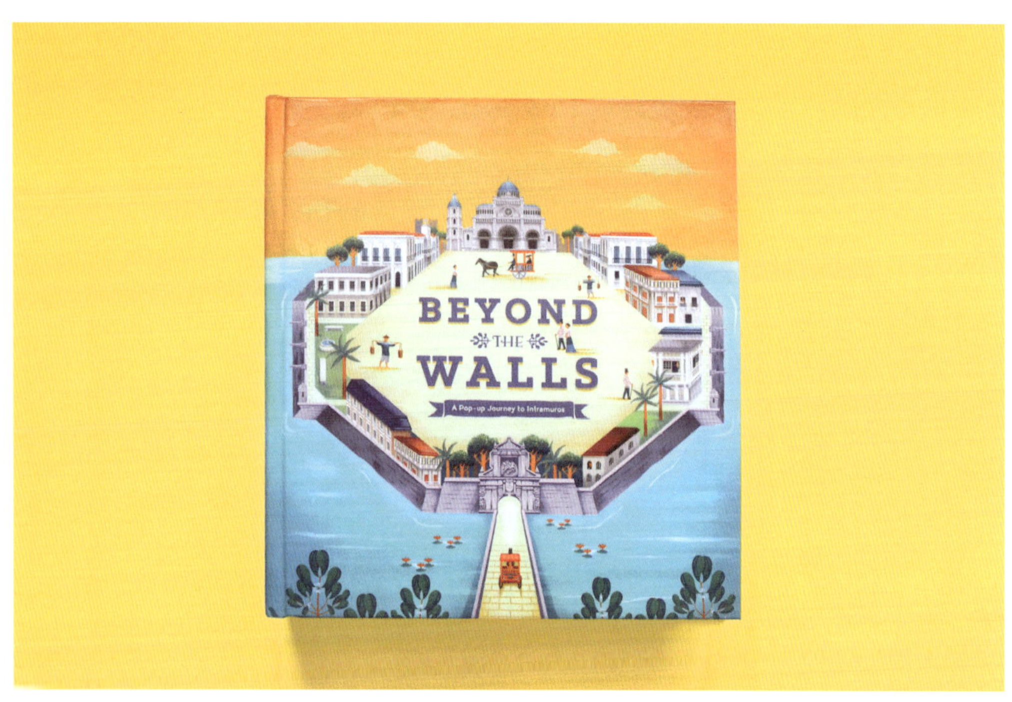

AGENTS OF EMPIRE

Aside from the walls, the Spaniards also built numerous churches to house the different friar orders that sailed to our country. These friar orders were priests who were devoted to different saints and converted the natives to Christianity. They built churches, schools, hospitals and convents. They also introduced the printing of books. Later on, some friars earned a bad reputation among Filipinos for their cruelty and corruption.

There were seven friar orders in Intramuros — the Augustinians, Dominicans, Franciscans, Jesuits, Capuchins, Recollects, and the Venerable Third Order — and each of them built their own church. The people of Intramuros would flock to these churches during Sundays and feast days at [illegible] side were intricate carvings, wall paintings, and life-size statues of saints.

The churches of Intramuros were not only home to the places of worship. They were also symbols of power and authority. As the Spaniards also used Catholicism to rule the Philippines, the churches became grand reminders of Spain's power.

1 - CEILING The ceilings of churches are painted with ornate designs.

2 - RETABLO This [illegible] carved shelf housing statues of the patron saint/s of the church

3 - ALTAR The altar is where the main mass service is carried out by the priest

4 - NAVE This is where the priest would walk going to the altar

5 - PULPITO This booth is where the priest gives his homily

6 - CAPILLAS These side chapels are dedicated to different saints and had smaller retablos

THE EMPIRE ARRIVES

Around the late 16th century, the Spaniards were sailing the world for new lands to conquer. And one of those lands is the Philippines.

Having heard of Maynila and its riches, they sent an expedition led by Martin de Goiti in 1570 to meet with Raja Sulayman. The expedition ended in a fiery battle. The following year, another expedition led by conquistador Miguel Lopez de Legaspi sailed to Maynila. Pressured by his elders, Raja Sulayman agreed for the Spaniards to take Maynila against his will.

And on May 19, 1571, Legaspi claimed Maynila for Spain, brandishing his sword in the air. From then on, Maynila would be known as Manila, and no more can the Tagalogs call it home. Maynila had become the city of the Spaniards, and it became the center of their government in our country.

The Tagalogs, meanwhile, crossed the river to the settlement of Tondo since their bustling port village had become somebody else's. And it was only the beginning. The Spanish Empire had just arrived.

INSIDE THE WALLS

Today, tourists and students stroll the cobblestone streets of Intramuros. But before, rich Spaniards, whirring calesas and glittering processions would pass by these streets.

Since there were eight churches around the city, the feast days of saints were big events wherein statues of saints or santos would be paraded around the streets. Everyone came out in their best garb to join the procession.

THE PLAZA MAYOR

The Plaza Mayor was Intramuros' heart. It was the center of all activites in the city. This was also were the most powerful - the church and government - were to be found. Eventually, the Spaniards applied the plaza to many other cities in the country, and up to this day, hundreds of Spanish-era plazas still exist.

AYUNTAMIENTO

The Ayuntamiento served as the city hall of Intramuros. It housed the offices of the civil governor and other city officials.

MANILA CATHEDRAL

The Manila Cathedral was home to the Archbishop of Manila. As head of the church, the Archbishop, whoever he was, was a major figure in the Philippines during the Spanish period. Today's cathedral is the sixth cathedral to be built on the site.

PALACIO DEL GOBERNADOR

This palace was the home of the Governor-General, or the head of government during the Spanish period. This was the predecessor of the Malacañang Palace.

Agathon's Apparatus

Designer
Emil Goozairow

Material
Luxury paper, cardboard, polymer clay, rope, hook

Size
65mm x 65mm

Completion
2015

Agathon's Apparatus consists of three pop-up pages that present Agathon's gear, instruments, and various devices found in the banks of the mysterious sea. The designer used a 'reverse illustration' method by making the drawings at the beginning of the design process and writing the stories at the end. Made of natural materials, such as wood, fabric, felt, and leather, the book is elaborately designed and has a unique appearance. The cover relief is made from polymer clay and bound with fasteners, ropes, and hooks.

Emil Goozairon
AGATHION'S APPARATUS
Description and history of
Rare and unique
instruments, apparatus and devices
from the Agathon Fazan's collection
DIALOGUES
TEXTS DESIGN BINDING BY
EMIL GOOZAIRON

3D Alphabet

Designer
Polina Artamonova

Size
240mm x 240mm

Completion
2014

'3D Alphabet' comprises a series of children's pop-up books that span the 32 letters of the Russian alphabet and present a wonderful world of magical characters and humanized animals. The designer made four volumes containing eight letters each and presented each letter as a three-dimensional paper pop-up. They are accompanied by a brief story and a short poem written by Russian poet Evdokia Kharitonovich to help children learn the alphabet. Polina Artamonova started with general ideas and sketches before making pencil-drawing illustrations of three-dimensional sketches.

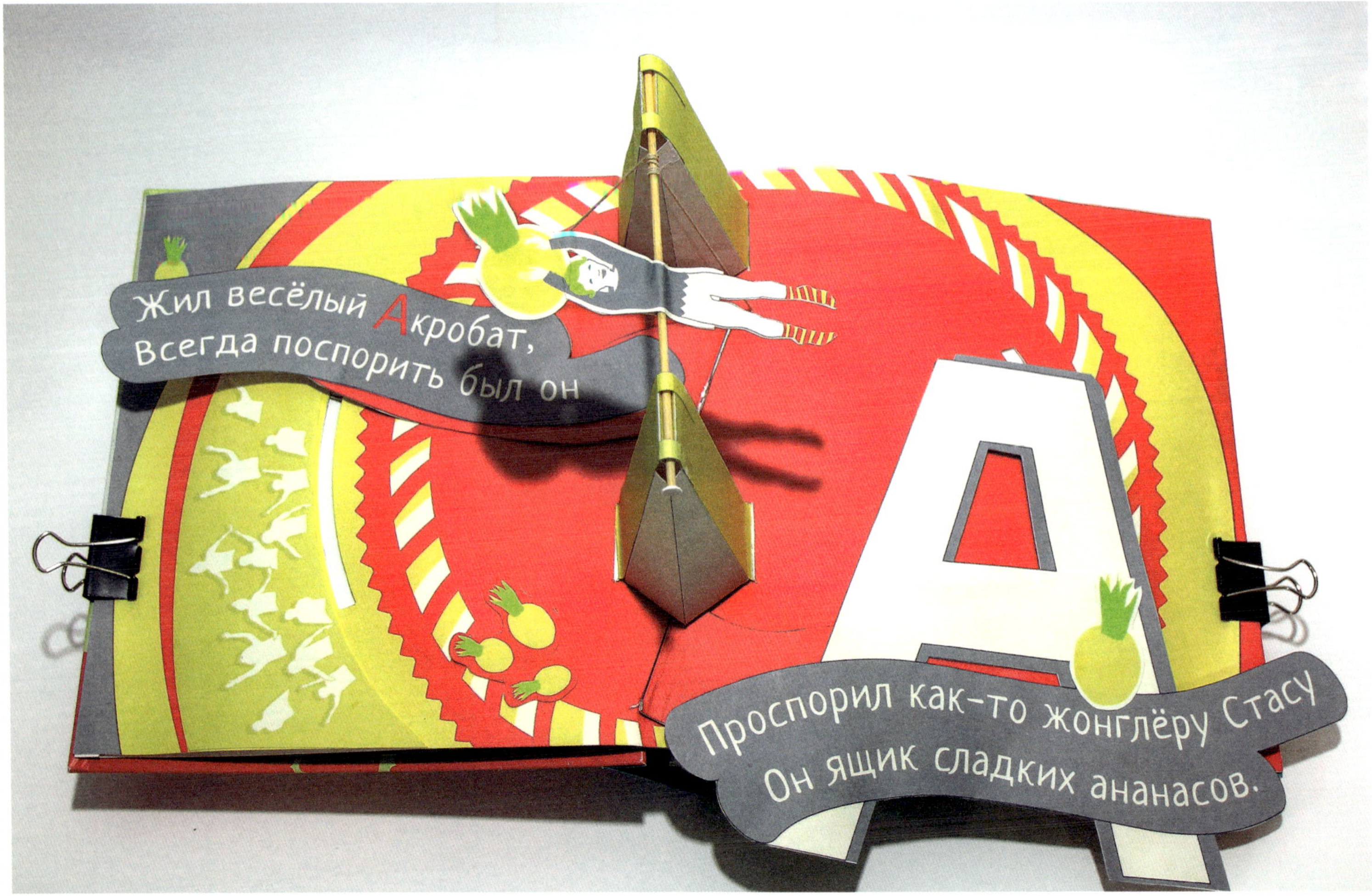

динорог
енный
Даже выйти он

ки, ды   ли
езд
В гости чтоб
ришлос

Жил в лесной избушке
маленький Барсук.
Он любил за книжками
Проводить досуг.

Живёт на свете старый Дед.
Дед тот добр, дед тот сед.
Любит делать он сюрпризы,
Путешествует без визы.

Кондрат
о рак
Тем, ч

кличке Соня
а спе
К виколо
шу озе

Лежал Тигр у камина,
Пил компотик из графина
И ногой качал вальяжно
Вид имея, важный.

Покрасила Русалочка волосы
В сине-бордовые полосы.
Под водой теперь ныряет,
Гордо хвостиком виляет.

Books of Spooks

Designer
Fanah Shapeless

Material
Paper, FIMO

Size
200mm x 200mm

Completion
2012

The interactive 'Book of Spooks' (*Kniha Strašidiel*) is about monsters. The designer asked children from the neighborhood to draw their vision of monsters and then used these images to illustrate the book. The designer wrote one story for each monster and made paper-craft toys that address different ways a child can play with a book. This includes pop-up elements and games, such as stickers, magnets, mirror foil, 3D monsters, paper dolls, and moving monsters parts, as well as an audiobook the designer's friends contributed to.

MODRÁK

V bukovom strome Strašidelného lesa sa celý život ukrývalo malé modré strašidlo Modrák. Občas síce vykuklo spoza kôry, aby nastrašilo nejakého turistu, ale len na chvíľočku. V kmeni stromu sa mu žilo dobre, malo veľa priestoru, kamarátilo sa s lykožrútmi a živilo sa bukvicami.

Nič mu vlastne nechýbalo, a preto je táto rozprávka o ňom úplne zbytočná. Veď, kto by stále chcel počúvať o tom ako je niekom tak dobre? Avšak pre istotu si dajte pozor, keď pôjdete najbližšie na turistiku, nezľaknite sa malého modrého strašidla, ktoré na Vás zareve spod kôry: „Bu-Bu-Bu."

44

SEDEMHLAVEC

Sedemhlavec mal sedem hláv a ako to už býva v rodinách s väčším počtom hláv zvykom, dochádza k viacerým rozporom, hádkam a občasným úderom. Najväčšia hlava by mala byť hlavná a tie menšie by sa jej mali podriadiť, lenže v tomto prípade boli menšie hlavy inteligentnejšie a nechceli poslúchať tú väčšiu a spolu mali oveľa viac rúk. Hlavy sa jednostaj ruvali, kričali po sebe, hrýzli sa a všetky tieto zvuky hádky a bitky stvorili povesť o strašidelnom lese.

Takže sa všetci tomu miestu vyhýbali a nikto nikdy spor siedmych hláv nevyriešil. Keby ste n náhodou prechádzali niekedy okolo, do Strašidelného lesa, zabehnite sedemhlavca, poklepte ho po ramene, pohlaďte ho po každej hlave a povedzte: „Všetko dobre dopadne, nemusíte sa hádať, naučím Vás kompromisom." a keby ani to nepomohlo, tak mu porozprávajte o výhodách a nevýhodách plastickej chirurgie.

35

What's Hiding in the Rainforest?

Designer
Nicole Yen

Material
Board, cloth, paper

Size
216mm x 279mm

Completion
2014

This interactive children's book gives a tour of the different critters that hide in the rainforests. Readers can wake a frog by rustling a leaf, coax a group of turtles out of their shells, or find a tapir amongst thick shrubs.

The design focuses heavily on the various camouflages of rainforest animals and insects and the paper engineering is based on the text. Readers can find and operate pull-tabs and flaps that reveal and disguise animals, as if in the wild.

THE ARRAU RIVER TURTLE
...TAMATA TURTLE is known for ...d and ridge-covered shell, long ... horns. His head is triangular and ... it has a number of projections, ...g an especially large horn on his ... His strange body resembles leaves ...ocks above the water.
...E SUNBITTERN has subdued feather coloration. When she needs to scare off predators or defend her territory, she opens her wings to reveal bright eye spots. Chicks are born active, and practice warning displays even before their feather markings appear.

The Lion King Fear

Designer
Cansu Öztürk

Printing Technology
**Matt cellophane coating
on hardcover**

Size
300mm x 480mm

Completion
2014

Cansu Öztürk adapted Sülayman Bulut's story 'The Lion King Fear' (*Aslan Kral Kork*) into a pop-up version. The designer used a digital illustration program and various paper textures to create a charcoal and halftone style. The text of the story is in Fertigo Pro font and the speech balloons and story title in VTKS Inked font. The designer highlighted words in the balloons to identify the lines said by the characters of the story.

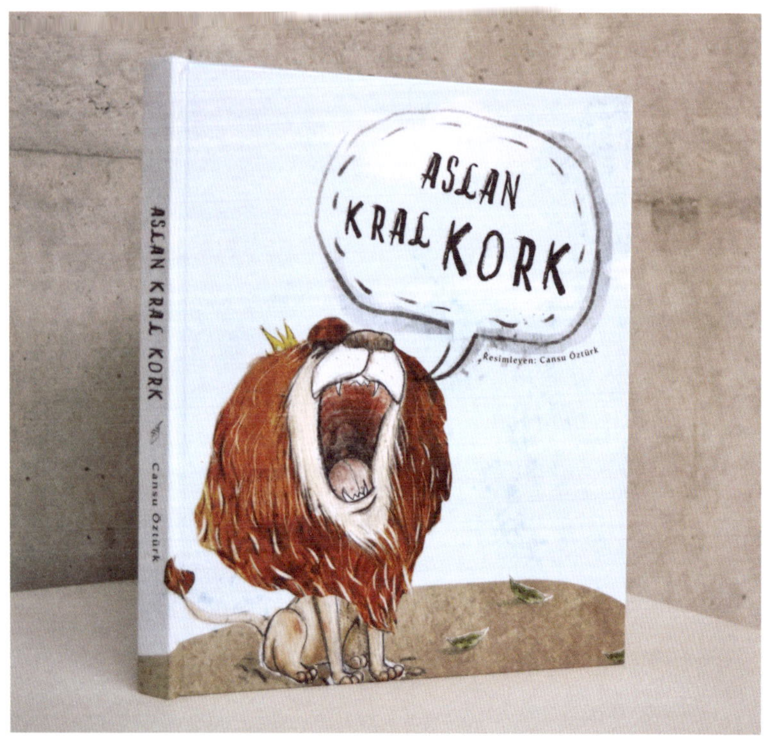

"Ne oldu Akkulak?"
"Seni kim korkuttu Akkulak?"
"Kimden kaçıyorsun Akkulak?"
"Neden konuşmuyorsun Akkulak?"
"Dilin mi tutuldu Akkulak?"

Akkulak, baktı ki soruların arkası kesilmeyecek, hepsine tek bir cevap vardı.

"Ormanda sahte bir kral dolaşıyor arkadaşlar!"

Birbirine baktı ötekiler. Ne vardı ...

"Ama kendini yeni kral olarak tanıtıyor," diye açıklamaya çalıştı Akkulak.
Kurt araya girdi.
"Değil mi peki?"
"Değil mi!! Sahte kral bu. Yalan söylüyor diyorum!"
Kısa bir sessizlikten sonra, aklıkirpi söze karıştı bu kez.
"Gerçek kral olmadığını nereden biliyorsun?" diye sordu.

DUYDUK DUYMADIK GÖRDÜK
GÖRMEDİK DEMEYİN İSTEEE
ASLAN KRAL KORK

Uzun ince gagasıyla yaprak üzerinde hızlı vuruşlar yapabilen ağaçkakan, Kral'ın buyruğunu aynen yazdı. "Yaz!" diye devam etti Kral Kork, "Yeni kralımız eski krallara benzemez, ondan korkulur...
Çünkü KIRK KULAĞI vardır.
Nerede, ne konuşursanız sizi işitir, ona göre!"

Tak, tik, tok...
Tik, tak, tik...

Kral'ın ikinci buyruğunu da noktasına, virgülüne dikkat ederek aynen yazdı ağaç-kakan. "Yazmaya devam," dedi Kral Kork, "yeni kralımız eski krallara benzemez, ondan korkulur... Çünkü KIRK PENÇESİ vardır.
Yanlış yapanı onun pençesinden hiçbir şey kurtaramaz, onlar cezasını bulur, ona göre!"

Son söylenenleri de yeşil yaprak üstüne hızla yazan ağaçkakan başını kaldırınca Kral Kork sordu:

"Tamam mı?"
"Tamamdır Sayın Kral Kork."

Ağaçkakan, bir yanlışlık yapmamak için tane tane okudu yazdıklarını. Onu dikkatle dinleyen Aslan Kral Kork, gururla başını havaya dikerek: "Bana çalıbülbülüyle papağanı çağırın," dedi.

Çalıbülbülüyle papağan uçarak geldiler. Bir kanatlarını açıp karınlarının üstüne koyarak kralı selamlayıp buyrukları için hazır olduklarını gösterdiler. Kral Kork, ağaçkakana dönerek buyrukların yazılı olduğu yaprakları çalıbülbülüne vermesini işaret etti. "Bütün ormanı ağaç ağaç gezecek; burada yazılanları yerde, gökte, suda yaşayan herkese okuyacak-sın," dedi. Çalıbülbülüyle papağan, haftalarca ormanı bölge bölge, ağaç ağaç gezip dolaştı.

Yeni kralın KIRK GÖZLÜ, KIRK KULAKLI, KIRK PENÇELİ olduğunu; her yapılanı gördüğünü; her konuşulanı duyduğunu; gücünün her an herkese yettiğini anlattılar.

Haftalar sonra geri dönüp, "Bütün orman sizin nasıl bir kral olduğunuzu çok iyi öğrendi kralım," dediklerinde yorgun ve bitkin durumdaydılar. Kral Kork onların bu durumlarını farketmedi bile. "Güzel!!" diye kükreyerek ayağa fırladı. "Şimdi sıra kendimi göstermeye geldi!"

Birinci baş yardımcısı
kısa boylu, uzun gövdeli,sivri burunlu tilki, kralın
hemen arkasında yürüyordu. İkinci başyardımcı, üçgen yüzlü,
sivri burunlu çakal da hemen yanındaydı. Çalıbülbülünün ne bağıracak sesi
ne kanat çırpacak gücü kalmadığı için kafilenin çığırtkanlığını, tek başına
papağan yapıyordu şimdi... Yorgun argın kanat çırpıyor, iyice kısılmış sesiy-
le orman halkına kralın ziyaretini duyurmaya çalışıyordu:

"YENİ KRALIMIZ ASLAN KRAL KORK...
SİZLERİ SELAMLIYOR!"

Papağanın sesini ilk duyan, Akkulak Tavşan oldu. Büyük bir böğürtlen
çalısının arkasında dinlenirken papağanın söylediklerini duyunca to-
parlandı hemen. KIRK GÖZLÜ, KIRK KULAKLI, KIRK PENÇELİ yeni kralı
çok merak ediyordu doğrusu.

Yola çıkıp selam durmadan önce,
yaklaşmakta olan krala doğru
baktı. Bir daha baktı.
Gözlerini ovuşturdu,
kapatıp açtı; bir
daha baktı. Bir
kulağını ileri doğru
uzatıp yeni kralın
gözlerini saydı;
bir, iki..
İki taneydi!

Birinci baş yardımcısı
kısa boylu, uzun gövdeli,sivri burunlu tilki, kralın
hemen arkasında yürüyordu. İkinci başyardımcı, üçgen yüzlü,
sivri burunlu çakal da hemen yanındaydı. Çalıbülbülünün ne bağıracak sesi
ne kanat çırpacak gücü kalmadığı için kafilenin çığırtkanlığını, tek başına
papağan yapıyordu şimdi... Yorgun argın kanat çırpıyor, iyice kısılmış sesiy-
le orman halkına kralın ziyaretini duyurmaya çalışıyordu:

"YENİ KRALIMIZ ASLAN KRAL KORK...
SİZLERİ SELAMLIYOR!"

Papağanın sesini ilk duyan, Akkulak Tavşan oldu. Büyük bir böğürtlen
çalısının arkasında dinlenirken papağanın söylediklerini duyunca to-
parlandı hemen. KIRK GÖZLÜ, KIRK KULAKLI, KIRK PENÇELİ yeni kralı
çok merak ediyordu doğrusu.

Kulaklarını saydı, o da iki taneydi. Pençelerini saydı, eh, o biraz fazlaydı;
dört taneydi. Kırk tane olduğu söylenen şeylerin hiçbiri kırk tane değildi.
Nasıl olurdu? Yaklaşmakta olan kralın sadece iki gözü, sadece iki kulağı,
sadece dört pençesi vardı..

Yanlış işitmiş olabilir miydi acaba?

Dikkatle, bir kere daha dinledi papağanı... Doğru duymuştu, "Yeni Kralımız!"
diye bağırıyordu papağan. Kırk gözü, kırk kulağı, kırk pençesi olmadığına
göre... Bu kral, yeni kral değildi. O zaman, papağan niye yeni kral olarak
tanıtıyordu onu? Tilki olsun, çakal olsun, yanındakiler de niye yeni kralmış
gibi davranıyorlardı ona? Ne demek oluyordu bu?

Yeni kral, böyle yaparak orman halkını sınıyor ol
Yalancıktan bir kral ortaya sürerek orman halkın
göstereceğini görmek istiyordu belki de!

Bir yanlışlık yapmak istemeyen Akkulak Tavşan,
krala karşı selam durmaktan vazgeçti. Böyle bir
öfkesini çekebilirdi çünkü. Onun kırk gözü vard
ne yaptığını hemen görürdü. İki gözlü, iki kulakl
kral önünden geçerken olduğu yere iyice büzüld
kayboldu Akkulak Tavşan.

Sinirlendi Akkulak. Karşı karşıya oldukları tehlike konusunda arkadaşlarını uyarmak istiyor ama kimseyi inandıramıyordu. Kısa kuyruğuyla sinirli sinirli havayı döverek:
"Evet, görmedik ama biliyoruz, değil mi?" diye sesini yükseltti. "Çalıbülbülüyle papağan bütün ormanı dolaşıp yeni kralımızın kırk gözlü, kırk pençeli, kırk kulaklı olduğunu söylemedi mi?"

"Eveeet," dedi ötekiler, birdenbire anımsamış gibi.
Akkulak devam etti:
"Bu kralınsa sadece iki gözü, iki kulağı ve dört pençesi var diyorum size... Kendi gözlerimle gördüm. Bu yalancı kral şimdi ormanda dolaşıp karşısında selam durmamızı istiyor! Ya gerçek kral bunu görürse? Kırk tane gözü var biliyorsunuz...

Akkulak konuştukça gözleri kocaman kocaman açıldı ötekilerin. Nasıl bir tehlikeyle karşı karşıya olduklarını sonunda anlamışlardı.

Derin bir soluk alan Akkulak, sözünü, şu uyarıyı yaparak tamamladı:
"Bu yalancı krala biz bir ders vermezsek gerçek kralın hışmından kurtulamayız."

Herkes çekingen ve şaşkın birbirine baktı. Uzun süren sessizliği bozan kurt oldu:
"Çok doğru... Bu yalancı krala selam durur, ona saygımızı sunarsak gerçek kralın öfkesini üzerimize çekeriz."

"Aaaaa," dedi sincap, aklına bir şey gelmiş gibi. Durdu, sağına soluna baktı: "Biz de saklanırız o zaman," diye devam etti ve fikrini açıkladı. "Karşısına çıkmayız, olur biter."

Başını sincaba doğru çevirdi kurt:
"Bir kere saklandın, iki kere saklandın... Bu sahte kral ormanda dolaştığına göre bir gün, bir yerde karşımıza çıkacaktır. Bence şimdi burada hep birlikteyken..."

Bütün kulaklar havaya dikildi. Kurt, konuşmasına devam ederek:
"Başımızı belaya sokmaya çalışan, kendini kral sanan bu krala bir ders verelim ki... Kimse bize bir daha böyle bir şey yapamasın!" dedi.

Ormanda yürüyüşüne devam eden Aslan Kral Kork, karşısındakilerin eğilmediklerini, saygı göstermediklerini görünce öfkelendi.

"Auuggrrrrrrr!" diye homurdandı. Kralın öfkelendiğini gören tilki hemen ilerleyerek en öndeki kurda:
"Yeni kralımız karşınızda dostlar! Yeni kralımızı selamlayalım ve bağımlılığımızı gösterelim ona!" diye seslendi.

Kurt, kararlı bir sesle cevap verdi:
"Biz, sadece Aslan Kral Kork'a bağlılık gösterir ve onu selamlarız."

"Beenn, Aslan Kral Kork!" diye kükredi Kral, topuzlu kuyruğunu sinirli sinirli havada sallayarak.

"Pışıkkk," dedi kurt, bir gözünü kırparak. Konuşmasına devam etti:

"Senin kaç gözün var?" diye sordu.

Aynı anda sivrisineklere bir işaret çaktı. Sivriler havalanıp bir anda, Kral[ın] etrafını sardılar. Önce sol, sonra sağ gözkapaklarının üs[tüne kon]dular. Kral Kork, önce "Aah!", sonra "Aahhhhh!" diye, [...] attı.

[...], ön ayaklarıyla ovuşturmaya [...] [k]urt: "Demek ki senin sadece iki gözün var," dedi.

"[...] Öyleyse sen Kral Kork değilsin!"

[...] [ar]kasından da:
"[... k]aç kulağın vardı? diye sordu. Sonra da [...] işaret çaktı. Arılar havalanıp iğnelerini, [...]['un] önce sol, sonra sağ kulağına batırdılar.

Fairy Tale Forest

Designer
Angelika Bujak

Material
Paper, cardboard

Size
210mm x 291mm

Completion
2015

'Fairy Tale Forest' (*Bajkowy Las*) is a series of six interactive books for children aged six to nine years old. The stories include 'Hansel and Gretel,' 'Puss in Boots,' 'Little Red Riding Hood,' 'Snow White,' 'Cinderella,' and 'Sleeping Beauty' and each book is in a different color to match the story. The books include three 3D illustration spreads inspired by theater along with a music CD and interactive elements related to the main characters.

Toys attached to the last pages of each book are intended to encourage children to interact with the stories in order to enrich their imagination. Angelika Bujak designed the books to appeal to children using bright and saturated colors, strong outlines, close compositions, and innovative patterns. The text is designed to be easy for children to read.

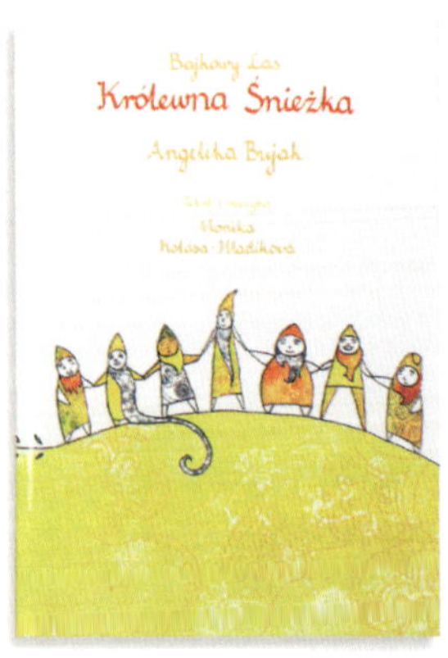

panereczka uśmiechnięta
i po drodze niech nie zwleka,
kiedy chora babcia czeka.

Drogie dzieci, czy Wy wiecie,
że wilk mieszka w internecie.
Czasem bestia ta zdradziecka,
umie mówić głosem dziecka.

Narrator:
Już wszystkie przyszły bajki, to ostatni taniec
Wszystkim dedykujemy nasze pożegnanie.

Ref.: Chodź z nami kolego do Lasu Bajkowego

Tu dziwy i cuda, piosenek sto do tego
W tym lesie wspaniałym bajki się spotkały,
I dzisiaj radośnie dzieciom zaśpiewały.

Narrator:
Witamy Jasia z Małgosią, nasi przyjaciele,
przeżyli kiedyś w lesie strasznych przygód wiele.

Żeby w podobnych chwilach wyjść obronną ręką,
rodziny, zapoznajcie się z naszą piosenką.

Narrator:
Witaj Królewno Śnieżko, witajcie krasnale
myślę, że nie trzeba Was przedstawiać wcale.

Także Wam poświęcimy dzisiaj trochę czasu
opowiemy, kto mieszka w domku w środku lasu.

Ref.: Chodź z nami kolego do Lasu Bajkowego...

Przyszedł także kot spryciula,
który za myszami hulał.
A gdy się z człowiekiem zbratał,
to z królewną go zeswatał.

Ref.: Chodź z nami kolego do Lasu Bajkowego...

Narrator:
Kot w butach przybył do nas,
witaj mości kocie.
Dziś u nas honorowe,
masz miejsce na płocie.
Wszyscy się bardzo cieszą obecnością Twoją,
nawet myszki zatańczą, choć się bardzo boją.

Bajkowy Las

Open Streets

Designer
Tayrine Cruz Carvalho

Size
220mm x 310mm

Completion
2012

'Open Streets' (*Pé Na Rua*) is an interactive and visual guide about museums and cultural places in São Paulo, Brazil. Tayrine Cruz Carvalho's goal was to make children feel welcome to visit each place and to teach them more about the culture of São Paulo.

The book has nine pop-up spreads and each page presents a dynamic illustration of the museum or cultural institution. A letter in the book summary identifies each place and its address and information is included on the relevant page. The designer used Base 12 and Sauna fonts and a color palette of black, white, gray, red, coral, yellow, and green to create an attractive universe for children and to stimulate their imagination.

MEMORIAL DA
AMÉRICA LATINA

Av. Auro Soares de Moura Andrade, 664 - Barra Funda
São Paulo, 01156-001

Conjunto arquitetônico desenhado por OSCAR NIEMEYER, o Memorial é caracterizado por ser um CENTRO CULTURAL, POLÍTICO E DE LAZER. Conta com um acervo permanente de obras de arte, um centro de documentação de arte popular latino-americana e uma biblioteca que possui cerca de 30 mil volumes, além da seção de músicas e imagens. O ambiente promove EXPOSIÇÕES, PALESTRAS, DEBATES, SESSÕES DE VÍDEO, ESPETÁCULOS DE TEATRO, MÚSICA E DANÇA.

Amazing Animal Alphabet

Designer
Pui Si Lo

Size
210mm x 210mm

Completion
2015

Amazing Animal Alphabet is a 26-page concertina pop-up book. Typically, pop-up books have a small number of pages because they can become too thick or difficult to publish. Therefore, a pop-up book like this one is rare to find. The designer selected unusual animals to differentiate it even further.

The concertina-style reflects the connections and stories between the animals and the designer believes it is a good way to read and understand the book, as children can open all the pages at the same time to relate the animals and stories together.

Z zebra

F frill-necked lizard
G gerenuk
hirola H

P
proboscis monkey
Q quail
red-lipped batfish R

Interactive
Books

Fun With Science

Designer
Dolnapa Jirungworapoj

Material
Coated paper, cardboard

Size
260mm x 285mm

Completion
2014

Dolnapa Jirungworapoj designed this pop-up book to create an interesting way for children to learn basic science in their everyday life. It has interactive elements and fun activities intended to make science theories easier to understand. Experimentation is a good method for children to learn and the book also contains six science experiments with necessary tools in a box set. The designer used paper-craft techniques and photographs for the illustrations to create a variety of textures, layers, and dimensions. Bright colors and rounded fonts give a playful and friendly aesthetic.

The Wind
in the Willows

Author
Kenneth Grahame

Designer
Anna Vahromejeva

Material
Cloth, 300gsm
watercolor paper,
140gsm recycled paper

Size
130mm x 205mm

Completion
2013

The story of The *Wind in the Willows* focuses on the life of four anthropomorphized animals: Mr. Mole, Mr. Rat, Mr. Badger, and Mr. Toad. Black-and-white pictures with fine lines reference the Edwardian tradition of the story. The book cover features a small minimalistic illustration of two main characters and green is used to represent nature. A butterfly pattern—created from a single illustration duplicated, scaled, and rotated—adds a subtle charm. The back cover is decorated with an image of a wooden frame that contains brief text and a hanging frog that references an episode of the story.

Each chapter is designated a special insect—bumblebees for the 'The River Bank' and a cockchafer for 'Mr. Badger'—and each page has the designated insect decorating the page numbers. The Goudy Old Style typeface is used for all text including the title. It comes with an activity book featuring modified line drawings of the book's illustrations for children to color. The rivet binding allows children to rotate sheets in any direction while the rest of the pages can be left for reference. Perforation makes it easy for children to tear out pictures and use them to decorate the walls.

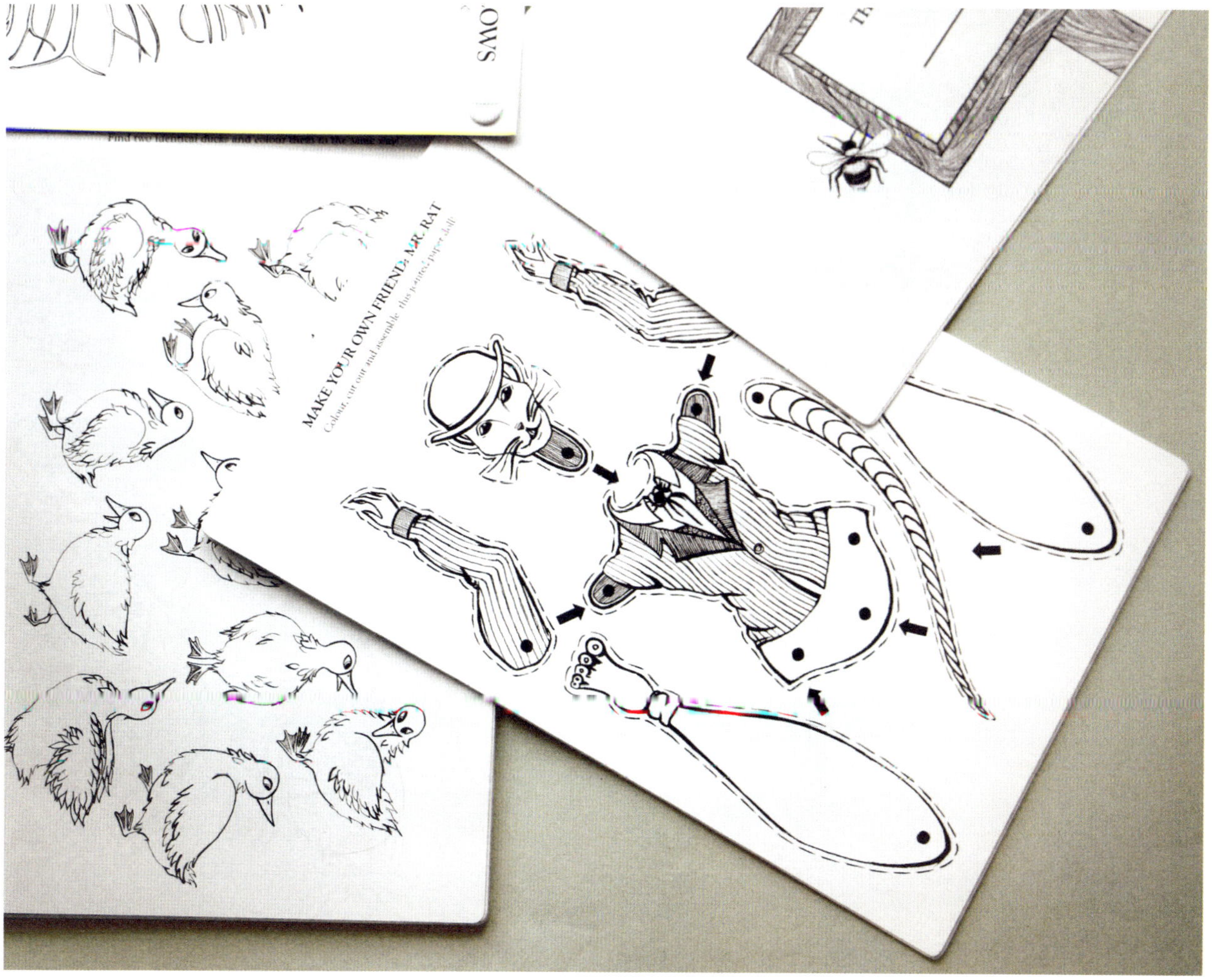

Find two identical ducks and colour them in the same way
MAKE YOUR OWN FRIEND MR RAT
Colour, cut out and assemble this paper-doll
WASHERWOMAN PAPER DOLL
Would Washerwoman in Mr Toad's clothes look as funny as he looks in hers?

But Noah
Is Waiting

Designer
Melanie Tonkowik

Material
250gsm and 160gsm BIO TOP 3®

Size
160mm x 190mm

Completion
2015

Melanie Tonkowik created 'But Noah Is Waiting' (*Aber Noah Wartet*) based on the story 'The Wolf and the Seven Young Kids' by the Brothers Grimm. The story is about seven children busily playing while their mother does the grocery shopping. All, that is, except the youngest child, Noah, who longingly waits for his mother's return.

The simple illustrations use limited colors to emphasize the interactive parts as well as the pop-up elements of this book. Readers are invited to interact with the children in the story by moving highlighted elements or turning pages. The book consists of 13 spreads and each has one line of text in German. The typeface is Ronnia by Type Together in 12pt, regular font.

Emma liest ein Buch.

Emma liest ein Buch.

Hannah kämmt sich die Haare.

Hannah kämmt sich die Haare.

Lara spielt mit Katze Nana verstecken.

Pauli isst eine Pizza.

Come & Play

Designer
Irina Schastnaya

Illustrator
Anna Silivonchik

Size
196mm x 236mm

Completion
2013

Publisher
AZ Books

Come & Play is a button sound book for young children with amusing and kind verses collected by Maryia Lysiuk. Anna Silivonchik did the illustrations and Irina Schastnaya designed the font of the headings. The illustrations are intended to be playful, ridiculous, and naive, as well as bright and colorful like children's drawings. The spectacular and picturesque illustrations were created using pencil sketches and oil paints on canvas, before being digitally processed.

Butterflies

Hush

Darkness Can Also Be Fun

Designer
Luisa Zamora

Material
Cardboard, artificial leather,
adhesive paper, printed fabric

Printing Technology
Gloss varnish

Size
275mm x 275mm

Completion
2014

'Darkness Can Also Be Fun' (*La Oscuridad También Puede Ser Divertida*) is an illustrated interactive book created to develop children's fine motor skills and to help them overcome the fear of darkness. The designer illustrated several characters to guide children's participation in various activities, which they can do alone or with others at bedtime. Each page is independent and the different activities are designed to improve children's specific abilities while they enjoy the experience of playing and learning.

COMPLETA EL CUERPO DEL MONSTRUO

DESCUBRE QUE HAY DETRÁS DE LA CORTINA

¡JUGUEMOS DENTRO DEL ARMARIO!

ADIVINA ¿QUIÉN ESTA DEBAJO DE LA CAMA?

Sum Fun

Designer
Lana Yassine

Material
PVC, cardboard, paper

Size
300mm x 300mm

Completion
2015

Sum Fun integrates art and games with fourth-grade math to improve children's learning and increase student attentiveness. The designer created 21 games and exercises based on lessons in the Grade 4 math book used in Lebanon.

The games and art exercises are add-ons to those already in the curriculum and are divided into four categories: problem solving, speed, drawing and painting, and collage. There are 10 games and 360 playing cards, two board games printed on fabric, 11 exercises, 15 templates on a CD, and stickers, pins, and awards that can be given to students to encourage them during the school year. A manual explains the details of games and exercises to teachers.

In addition, *Sum Fun* provides a website that is both a blog and a forum for teachers to share what is happening in their classes, to ask other teachers who are using the *Sum Fun* box questions, as well as to give each other tips.

WHAT'S THE HIDDEN IMAGE?
CONNECT THE DOTS!

5.2   1.4   6.7   1.6
9.1   5.8   2.1   4.2
3.5   6.2   1.2   12.4
1 CHOSE THE SCOOPS THAT ADD UP
   TO THE NUMBER ON THE CONE.
2 SHOW YOUR TEACHER.
3 CUT OUT THE SCOOPS AND THE
   CONE AND GLUE THEM TOGETHER!
HAVE FUN!

SUM FUN
SNOW
BOARDING
DIVISION
SNOW
BOARDIN

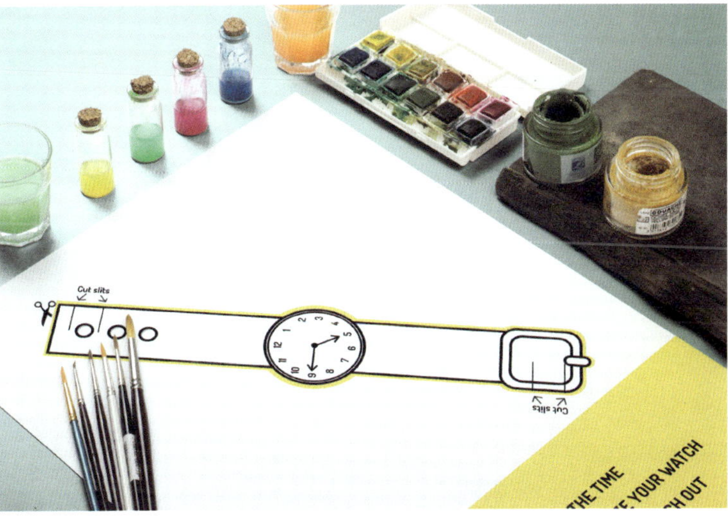

Cut slits
Cut slits

The Strange Footprint!!

Designer
Pin Shuan Chen

Size
220mm x 305mm

Completion
2015

The Strange Footprint!! is about a boy named Arthur who doesn't care about the environment and energy waste. The designer used a broad color palette. There is an element, such as the monster or footprints, to find on most of the pages. Children can learn about emotions and facial expressions from the Carbon Monster's face and can gain a greater understanding about the concept of the carbon footprint by using fun ways to learn, including an interactive picture book and a board game at the end of the story.

"

And the detective discovered clues revealing a carbon monster had been at large!

The detective discussed with Arthur ways in which he could reduce his "carbon footprint" by changing his life style!!

Arthur is a boy who is always creating energy waste and does not have any idea about protecting the environment.

One day, Arthur wakes up and he finds a letter on the table addressed to him.

SEW: Saving Endangered Wildlife

Designer
Mirim Seo

Size
345mm x 470mm

Completion
2012

SEW: Saving Endangered Wildlife is a game to teach children about endangered rainforest species as well as hand-sewing techniques by completing sewing patterns of endangered rainforest animals. *SEW* has eight levels of difficulty and includes an instruction book and eight animal pieces with stitch holes for easy assembly; plus children can create their own animal designs.

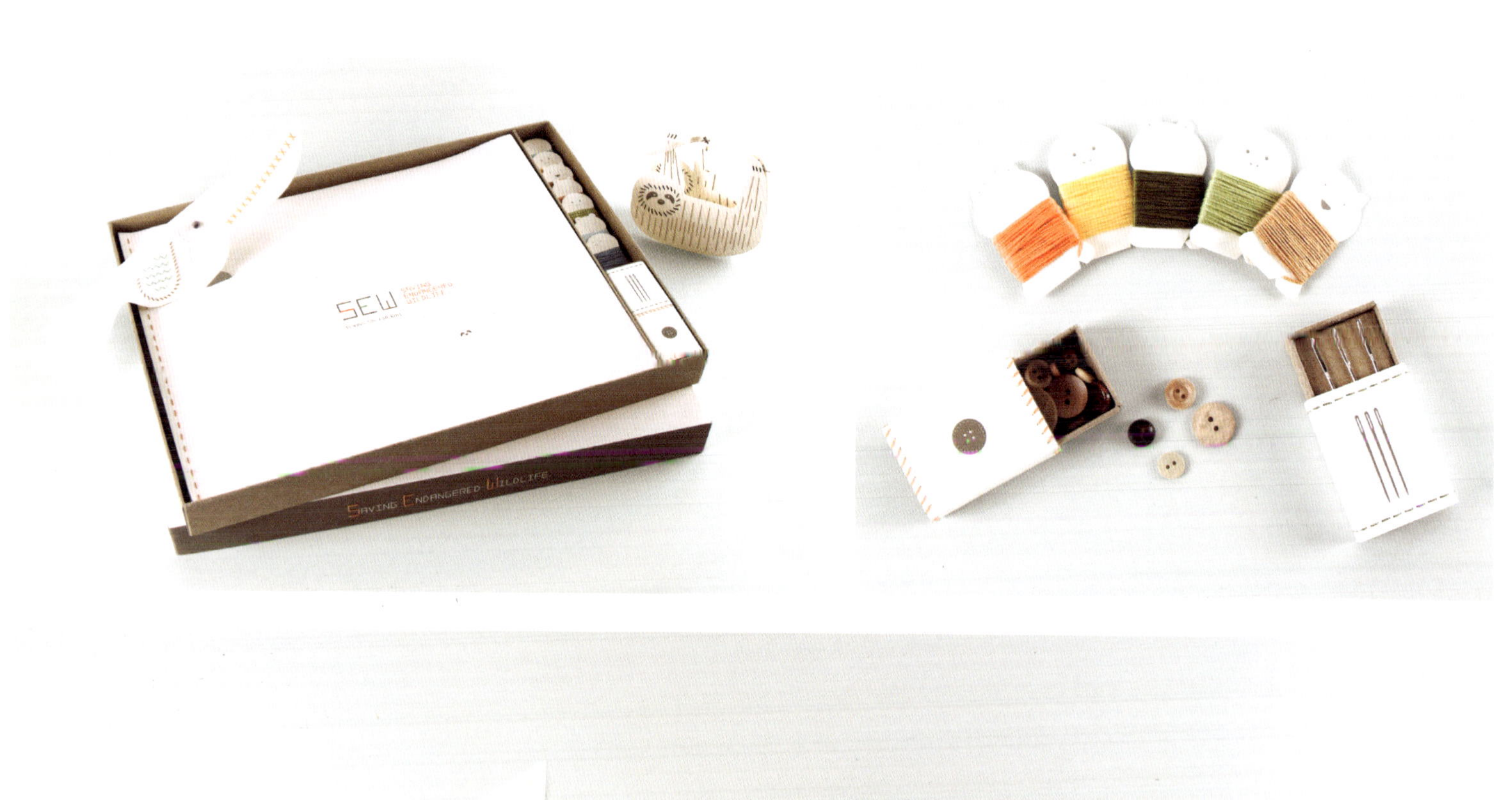

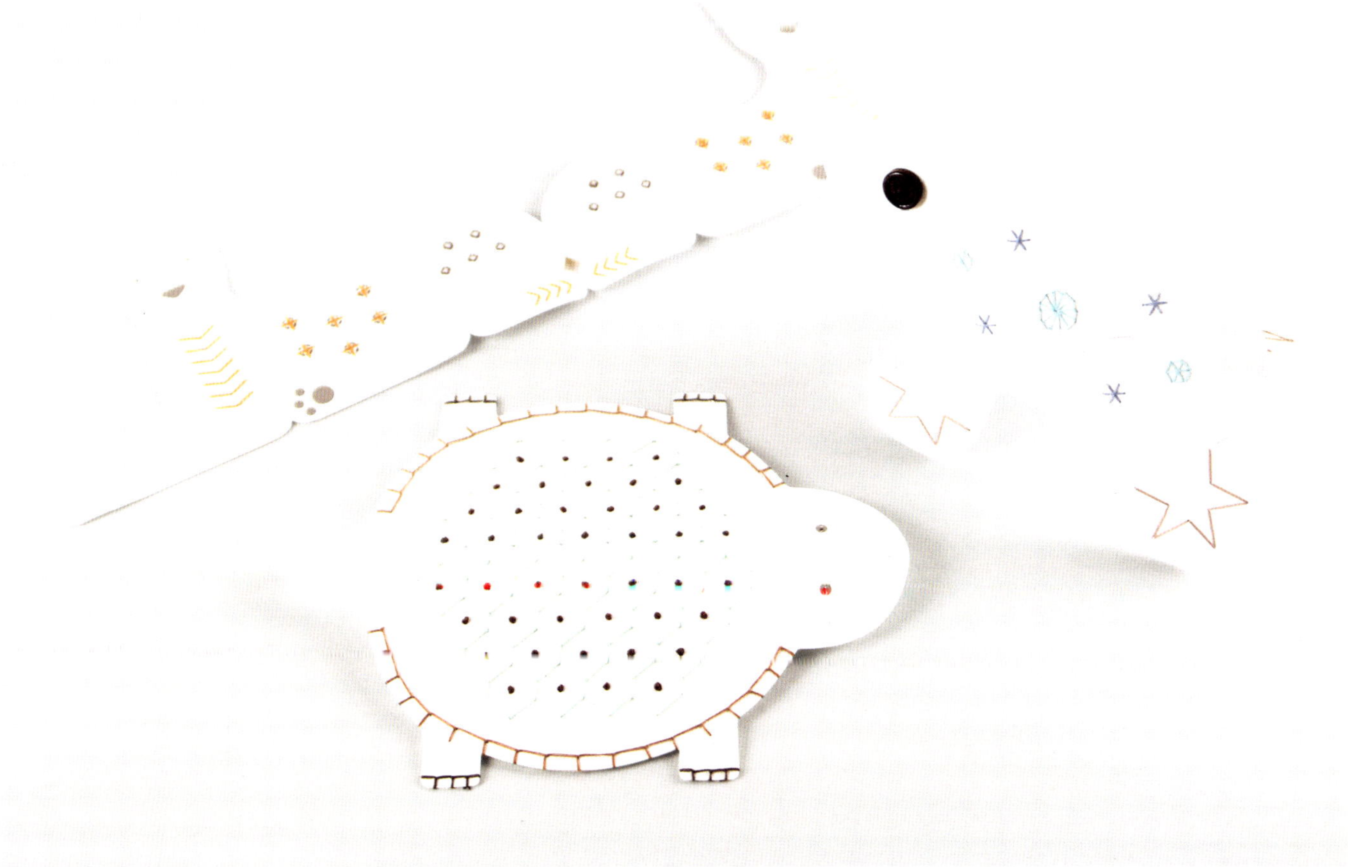

Ready, Set, Go!

Designer
Marianna Balducci

Size
200mm x 200mm

Completion
2014

Publisher
Unione di Prodotto Costa

'Ready, Set, Go!' (*Pronti, Partenza, Via!*) is a coloring-in book produced for a tourism group to promote the Adriatic coast during the Children's Festival in Emilia Romagna. The story is a treasure hunt in which two children and their dog spend holidays at the Adriatic coast and discover different and wonderful things about the place before they find the final treasure, the Adriatic Sea. The book is a welcome guide for visitors as well as being full of content and games for children aged between five and ten years old. It has a smart format that is easy for children to carry.

RAVENNA

Ritrovata la giusta ... da, la storia spalanca i suoi portoni. '...silica di E.Vitale...' legge 'questo sì che sembra un posto pieno di tesori!'

Costruita in epoca bizantina, S.Vitale è piena di mosaici e uno raffigura persino l'imperatore Giustiniano che però sembra avere qualche problema con tutte quelle tesserine...

Con questa storia dei mosaici mi sento tutto scombinato...

AIUTA GIUSTINIANO A TROVARE IL PEZZO GIUSTO

LE PAROLE CORRONO VELOCI!

ISOLA SOLO QUELLE CHE HANNO UN SENSO CERCHIANDOLE CON LA MATITA

LE SPIAGGE DI RAVENNA

CERVIA

MILANO MARITTIMA

'La vedi?' si chiedono l'un l'altra cercando la mappa nella variopinta sfilata di trabaccoli e bragozzi ormeggiati al museo della marineria di Cesenatico. Le barche risalgono alla fine dell'800 e all'inizio del '900, ma alcune di loro sono ancora in grado di navigare.

FORLÌ - CESENA

TROVA LA MAPPA CHE SI È PERSA (pagina precedente). Poi INVENTA E COLORA ALTRE VELE

Le vele sono tutte diverse, decorate con simboli e disegni che ricordano le antiche famiglie di pescatori romagnoli. Hanno una forma a trapezio e si chiamano vele al terzo per via del modo in cui sono posizionate sulla barca.

CESENATICO

GATTEO A MARE

SAVIGNANO MARE

SAN MAURO MARE

I Am Going to Think About It

Designer
Inês Fonseca

Material
**120gsm matte
white paper**

Size
195mm x195mm

Completion
2015

Publisher
**Alêtheia Editores
and Pingo Doce**

'I Am Going to Think About It' (*Vou Pensar Nisto*) is a series of 10 children's books that combine play with serious issues such as freedom, hope, courage, friendship, and family. It aims to help children learn important values in a fun and colorful way.

As the project explores different perspectives and points of view—just like a child's mind—so too the illustrations and layouts are designed to be as free as possible. Every page surprises readers with varied and appealing colors that strongly contrast with the white of the main character, which becomes a blank canvas for children to paint. At the end of each book, children are challenged to return to the pages of the book to discover hidden details such as candies, bugs, and fruits.

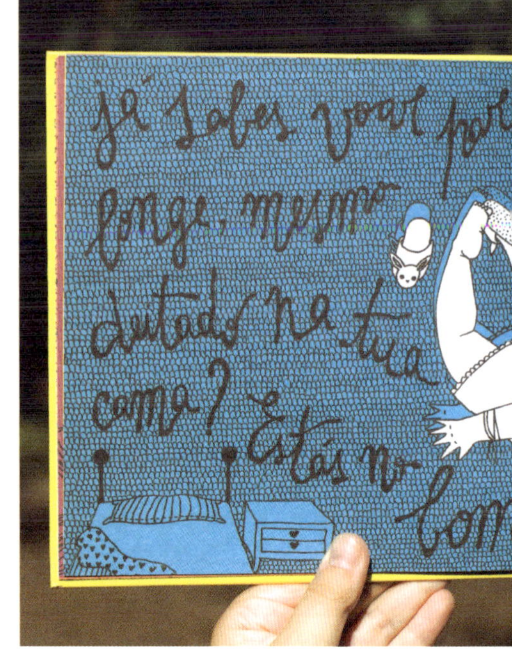

e as jóias da
família
valem mais
do que as
da coroa

aminho para encontrar
a
liberdade

ter esperança é como
ter uma   manta
numa   noite fria

Chasing Words

Designer
MingHsi Mish Chou

Material
Wool felt, paper, velcro

Size
254mm x 254mm

Completion
2014

'Chasing Words' (*Boj o Poklad*) is a storytelling set that includes an illustrated paper book, a pop-up interactive felt book, and a playable vest. The set is designed to promote talking and understanding for children with communication disabilities and imagination difficulties.

Animals and fruits can be added and removed from the book to encourage children to tell their own stories and enhance their interaction with the activity. The vest is intended to help children identify story time. Since children are easily distracted, the designer created a vest based on Deep Pressure Therapy to help children relax and concentrate.

nrrr~

Elephant is
scared

CHOMP:
Food Chain
Puzzle Books

Designer
Mirim Seo

Material
Paper, wood

Size
145mm x 215mm

Completion
2012

The CHOMP project is a series of five books designed to teach children about the basic food chain. The designer made the book like a puzzle to encourage children to learn in a playful manner and every character is cute and interesting. The puzzles introduce different levels of the food chain in different environments such as the forest, ocean, arctic, jungle, and desert. The puzzles are made of wood so as not to be broken easily and the puzzle shows the eating process when completed.

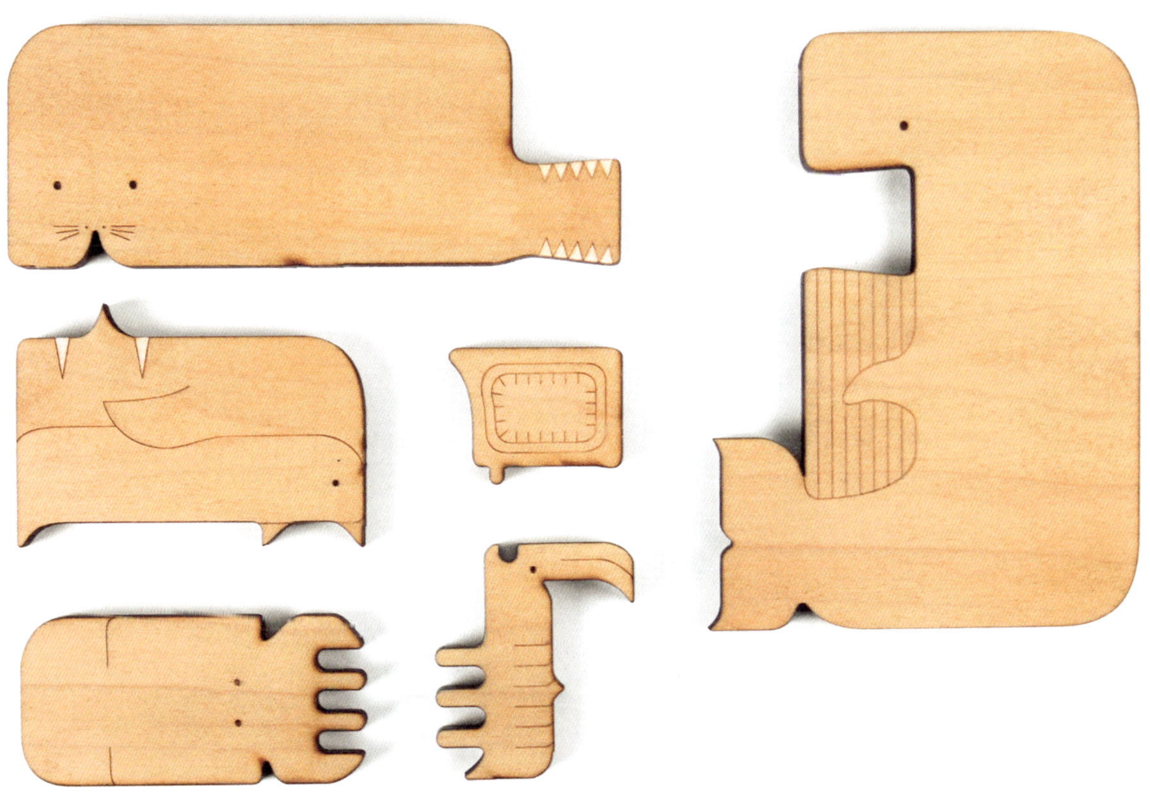

Battle for Treasure

Designer
Fanah Shapeless

Material
Paper, wood

Size
160mm x 200mm

'Battle for Treasure' (*Boj o Poklad*) is for older children. Children can read the story and then play the games in the book. It combines the principles of the English game Ludo with a fairy tale, which can be used as a walkthrough of the game.

Children can choose to be a prince, princess, or very friendly monster. The prince is searching for the golden treasure hidden in the monster's cave; the princess is looking for her chosen prince in the castle; and the monster wants to find a pantry full of food and a bed for sleep. The game is intended to help children understand and remember the story easily and stimulate their imagination and activity.

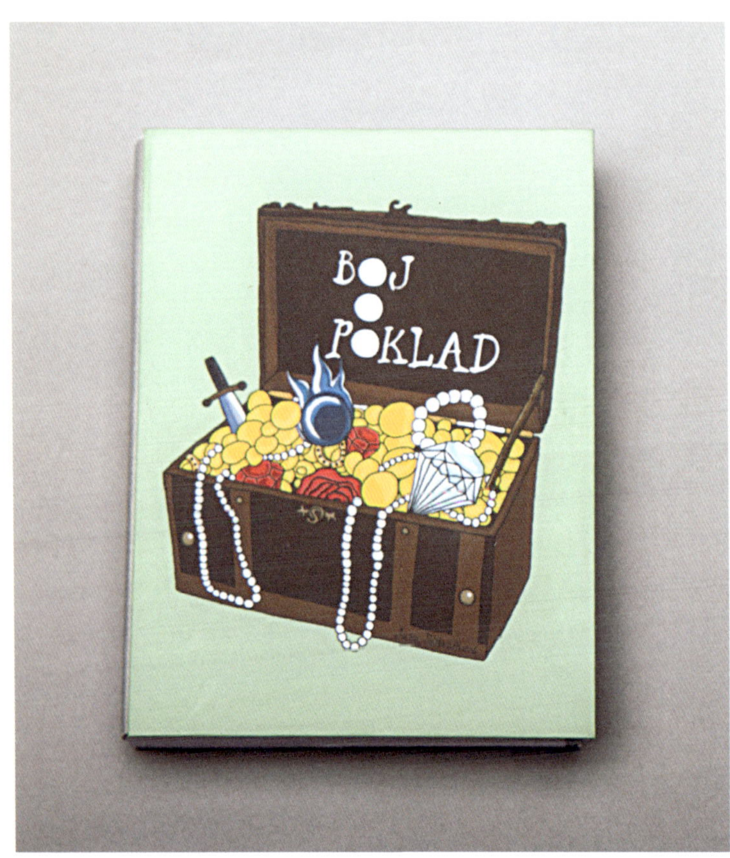

My Out the Back Pack

Designer
Aleisha Findlay

Material
Ribbed synthetic fabric,
card, magnetic metal clasps,
magnifying glass,
wooden pencils

Size
165mm x 225mm

Completion
2014

My Out the Back Pack is an adventure kit that aims to encourage children aged six to eight years old to engage in outdoor and creative play, practicing skills that can contribute to their well-being, and balancing out their time spent using technology.

The book provides children with funny, interactive backyard activities designed to get them exploring their outside environment. It has die cuts and pockets to store collected items as well as spaces for children to draw, write, and add their own personalized touches. The use of freehand typography throughout the book creates a crafty and tactile feel.

BACKYARD SAFARI

With your fellow explorers can you find these little crawly creatures in the following picture?

Two snails, five ants, one butterfly and one caterpillar

Can you discover some of these crawly creatures on your own backyard safari? Using a magnifying glass you can them look at them more closely.

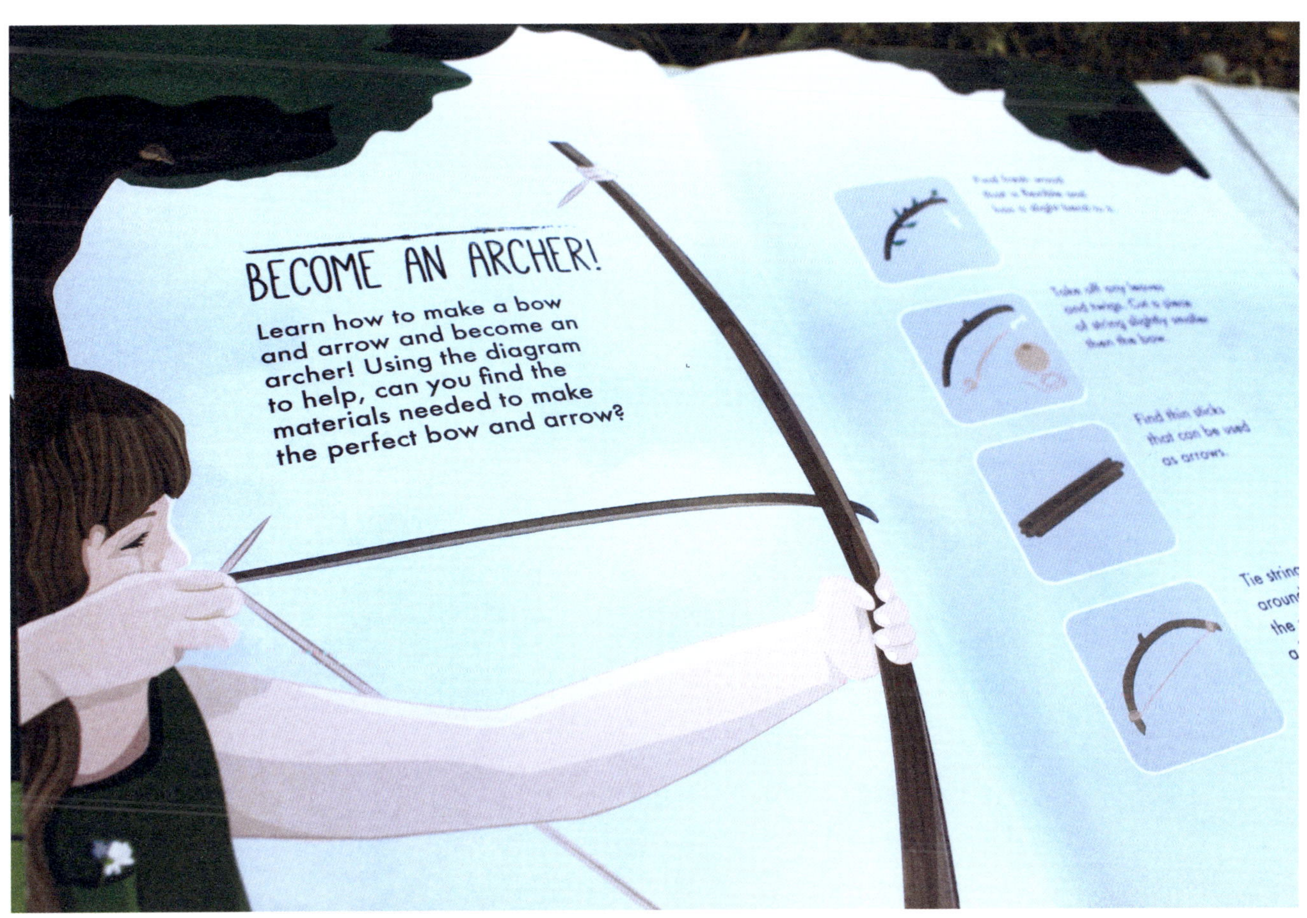

BECOME AN ARCHER!

Learn how to make a bow and arrow and become an archer! Using the diagram to help, can you find the materials needed to make the perfect bow and arrow?

4 DEALING WITH FEELINGS
Face your fears in a
bear hunt adventure!
Day dream and laugh at
the funny shaped clouds
Don't be afraid to get
messy and create muddy
fingerprint pictures
Peering into tree
hollows makes for
an exciting adventure

TREE CLIMBING

DAISY CHAINS
Hunt them on the lush green
grass for daisies. Pick as
many as you can find (being
sure to pick them with lovely
long stems) and collect them
in a bag or basket. Now
you can make your very own
daisy chain! What can you
make your daisy chain into?

MUD PUDDLES
your muddy
hand print here!

SECRET GARDEN
Plant your own
secret garden!

You will need a pot and
some soil. Place the soil
into the pot, fill almost to
the top.

You will need seeds to start
growing your secret garden!
Poke three seeds down into
the soil in different spots.

Now you can watch your
plants grow! Tomato plants
will start to sprout after a
week. Place your pot in a
sunny place and make sure
you give it water when the
soil is no longer damp.

CUP PHONES
Make your own cool
phones out of plastic cups!

You will need two plastic
cups to make your phones.
Thread string through the
holes made in the bottom
of each cup and tie a knot
from the inside.

You will need some string
for the phones cord and
scissors to poke holes into
the bottom of the cups.

Thread string through
the holes made in the
bottom of each cup and
tie a knot from the inside.
Now you can chat from
distances with your fellow
explorers!

Arturo

Designers
Anna Masini, Bruaá Editora

Size
158mm x 256mm

Completion
2012

Publisher
Bruaá Editora

The design of *Arturo* emphasizes the slow, dramatic rhythm of the story and underlines its poetic, contemplative side. The designers used a simple format to give children an opportunity to be immersed in the narration without superficial distractions and to balance the images and words for a harmonious and coherent structure.

A basic binding and hardcover gives a bright, light character to the wistful, even dark, atmosphere of the story. The horizontal frames determined the dimensions of the book, as did the content of the story: as long as a dachshund, as stretched as the handmade fabric puppet, and as wide open as the suspended plot.

Pensei perguntar à senhora onde compras sempre o pão se ela te tinha visto. Não tinha

Onde é que foste?

… aquele canto do parque onde gostavas de ficar a ler…

Colour in Oakham

Designer
Deborah Pow

Size
210mm x 297mm

Completion
2014

This illustrated coloring-in book is filled with activities for children attending an English summer school based in Oakham, England. It won the Design in Action Prize for Commercial Potential 2015. The center of the book holds ABC Snap cards using an alphabet made up of things to be found in Oakham and the activities and excursions the students take part in. The cards are designed to help children learn simple English words and to make friends by teaming up with partners, as well as encouraging them to play the game Snap and to color-in during their spare time.

The book includes drawing activities, dot-to-dot games, spot the difference, postcard designing, and illustrated maps of Oakham and the Alton Towers theme park, which the students visit on an excursion. The back of the book also contains stickers that children can swap with their new friends. Specific colors on each page indicate the best location for each activity.

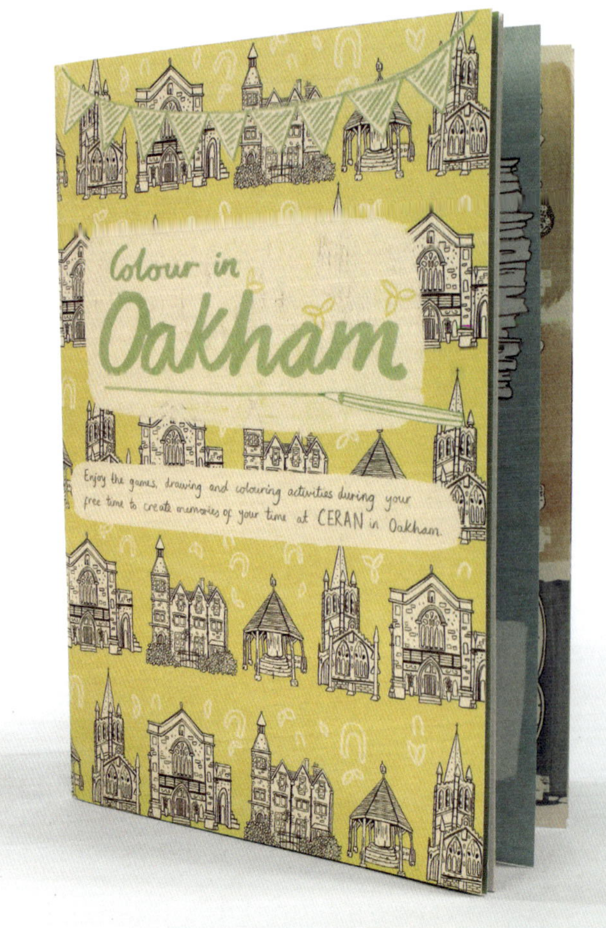

Art Sculptures
Oakham Castle
Collect materials and make your own sculpture of an animal.
DRAW YOUR SCULPTURE HERE
Located at the
on your MAP
* USE YOUR MAP TO FIND THE CASTLE *
THERE ARE ☐ HORSE SHOES IN THE CASTLE.
Why is the HORSE SHOE the symbol of Oakham?
Draw the other half of the Castle wall

Rutland Falconry and Owl Centre
Draw the owls in their correct places!

* ASK AN ACTIVITY LEADER IF YOU NEED HELP *
Write th   nds or parents here
Write your message here
BOOKMARK
Oakham
FERAN
YORK MINSTER
Draw the other half of York Minster with help from the numbers!

Cambridge
University of Cambridge
PEMBRONE COLLEGE
Kings College
MATHEMATICAL BRIDGE
Bridge of Sighs
COLOUR AND DRAW
Cambridge Architecture
My favourite building was
THE ROUND CHURCH

The map of
Oakham
STATION ROAD
STATION ROAD
KILBURN
PARK LANE
OVERTON R
NORTHGATE ST
NORTHGATE ST
FINKEY ST
CHURCH ST
BURLEY ROAD
LONG ROAD
NEW STREET
JOHN ST
GOAL ST
HIGH STREET
HIGH STREET
MARKET PLACE
MILL STREET
SOUTH STREET
The horseshoe is the symbol of Oakham
Built for the smallest man in England
Where villagers would buy produce in Medieval times
Open Wednesdays and Saturdays
KEY:
1. Train Station
2. Hudsons Cottage
3. Signal Box
4. Oakham School Chapel
5. Oakham School
6. Butter Cross and Pump
7. Oakham Castle
8. Oakham Band Stand
9. Police Station
10. All Saints' Church
11. Tennis Courts
12. Dinner Hall
13. Art Studio
14. Oakham Market

Children's Quiet Book

Designer
Elena Khodatska

Material
**Fleece, felt, zipper, cotton,
denim, beads, ribbons,
laces, fabric**

Size
210mm x 180mm

Completion
2015

Publisher
MiniMom's

These quiet activity books made of cloth are recommended for children aged one year old and over. Different clasps on each page include velcro, buttons, knobs, shoelaces, zippers, pins, and yarn. Thick pages enable the book to stand upright and encourage children to develop the use of their hands. With the help of this book, children can learn colors, geometric shapes, figures, and counting, and parents can help teach their children the concept of size—small, little, short, big, and long.

Grow

<table>
<tr><td>Author</td><td>Allison Khoury</td></tr>
<tr><td>Design Agency</td><td>Sequence</td></tr>
<tr><td>Designers</td><td>Karin Bryant, Leslie Wang, Tammy Chang</td></tr>
<tr><td>Material</td><td>Matte paper, custom stickers</td></tr>
<tr><td>Size</td><td>216mm x 280mm</td></tr>
<tr><td>Completion</td><td>2012</td></tr>
<tr><td>Publisher</td><td>Chipotle Mexican Grill</td></tr>
</table>

Sequence designed and produced this children's activity book for Chipotle Mexican Grill and it features fun and educational activities to teach kids where food comes from and how it grows. Children can learn about the different parts of fruit and vegetables, stages of plant life, farming, and composting.

The book features freehand typography, original illustrations, and a character named Steve the Seed that guides children through the activities in the book. The majority of the book was kept black and white to encourage coloring-in. Children can also do longer projects on the take-home activities page. An integrated folder on the last page holds stickers, recipe cards, and a packet of tomato seeds.

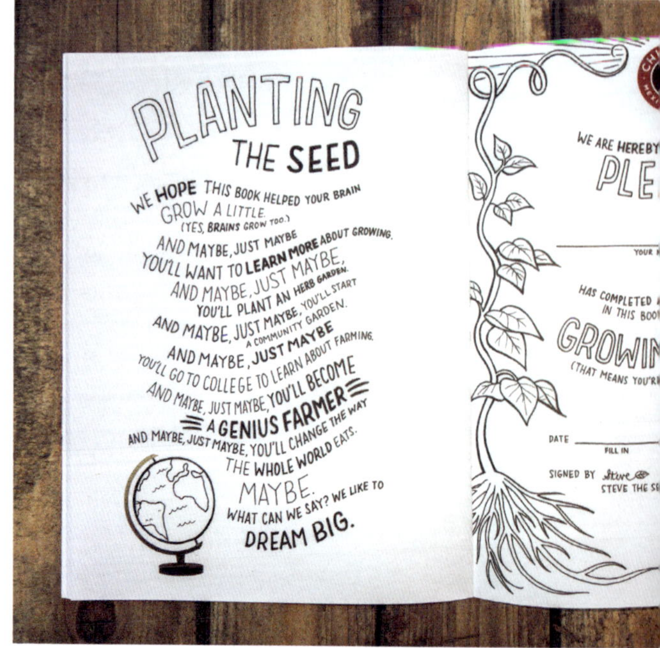

THAT
ITIES
RU
SMART.)
CONGRATS
I'M SO PROUD
OF YOU.

PLANT POWER
PLANTS STORE ENERGY
IN THEIR LEAVES, ROOTS,
FRUIT, STEMS AND SEEDS.
WHEN YOU EAT THESE PARTS
OF THE PLANT, THE ENERGY
IS PASSED ON TO YOU.
YOU GET MORE ZIP.
MORE ZING.
MORE POW.
PSSST
PLANTS HAVE
ENERGY.
PASS IT
ON
FRUIT
LEAVES
STEM
SEEDS
ROOTS
WHAT PART OF THE PLANT ARE YOU EATING?
DRAW A LINE FROM THE FOOD TO THE PLANT PART.
LEAVES
ROOTS
FRUIT
STEMS
SEEDS

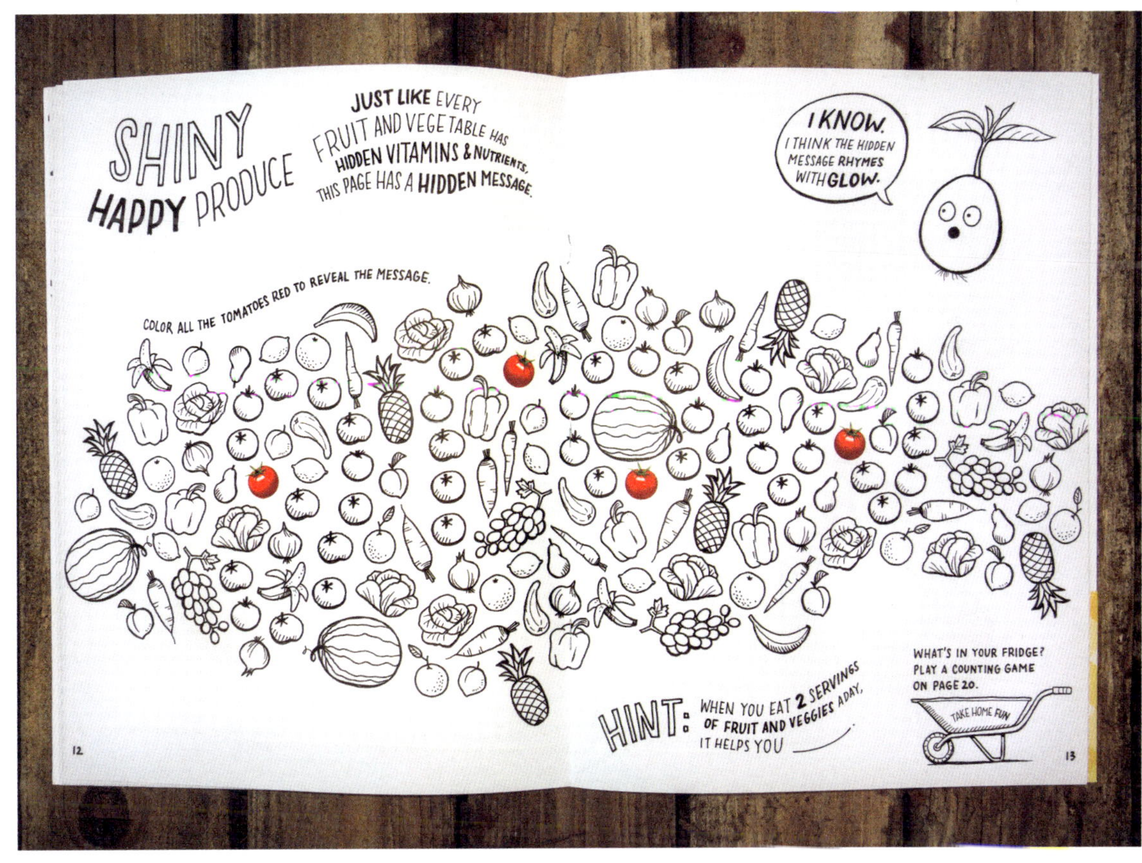
SHINY HAPPY PRODUCE
JUST LIKE EVERY
FRUIT AND VEGETABLE HAS
HIDDEN VITAMINS & NUTRIENTS,
THIS PAGE HAS A HIDDEN MESSAGE.
I KNOW.
I THINK THE HIDDEN
MESSAGE RHYMES
WITH GLOW.
COLOR ALL THE TOMATOES RED TO REVEAL THE MESSAGE.
HINT: WHEN YOU EAT 2 SERVINGS
OF FRUIT AND VEGGIES A DAY,
IT HELPS YOU ____
WHAT'S IN YOUR FRIDGE?
PLAY A COUNTING GAME
ON PAGE 20.
TAKE HOME FUN
12
13

Leica Activity Book

Design Agency
Halfazebra Studio

Printing Technology
UV varnish

Size
180mm x 260mm

Completion
2014

Publisher
Leica Camera Inc.

Halfazebra Studio designed this activity book for the children of customers browsing the Leica Camera store. It includes coloring-in pages, mazes, word searches, and other games. The design is simple with a minimalistic layout, short sentences, and clean camera illustrations that encourage children to be the artist. In this way, children can express their creativity and learn about Leica's products and its history.

NOW A LITTLE HARDER.
GET TO THE OTHER SIDE
COMPLETE THE X2 MAZE ON THE RIGHT
us.leica-camera.com

A NEW FORM
THE SENSATION OF 1964
The Leicaflex was Leica's first 35mm
single-lens reflex camera.
LEICAFLEX
us.leica-camera.com

Ada's Quiet Book

Designer
Kristy Kaufer

Material
Felt, fabric, bead, button, sequin

Size
152mm x 229mm

Completion
2012

Enthralled by her daughter's imagination and stories, Kristy Kaufer designed *Ada's Quiet Book* for her three-year-old daughter. Many of the designs are based on the stories her children told, the games they made up, and the dreams they relayed. Each page is a simple scene that serves as a starting point for children to create their own imaginative story. The book is made of high-quality wool felt and fabrics and the designer sewed and embroidered each part of the book by hand, preferring the look of hand-stitching to machine-stitching.

Ilustrated Harry Potter

Author
J. K. Rowling

Design Agency
Zaloom

Illustrator
Werllen Holanda

Material
Cover: 120gsm high brightness paper
Leaves: 180gsm high brightness paper

Printing Technology
Hot stamping

Size
240mm x 275mm

Completion
2014

Publisher
Zaloom

This book features pop-ups and illustrations adapted from J.K. Rowling's *Harry Potter and the Philosopher's Stone*. Zaloom designed the project because no printed product of the Harry Potter brand existed for younger audiences. The spreads consist of two columns of text on the far side of each page and illustrations in the remaining space. Pop-ups and other interactive features, such as a letter from Hogwarts, are included to make children's experience with the book as engaging as possible.

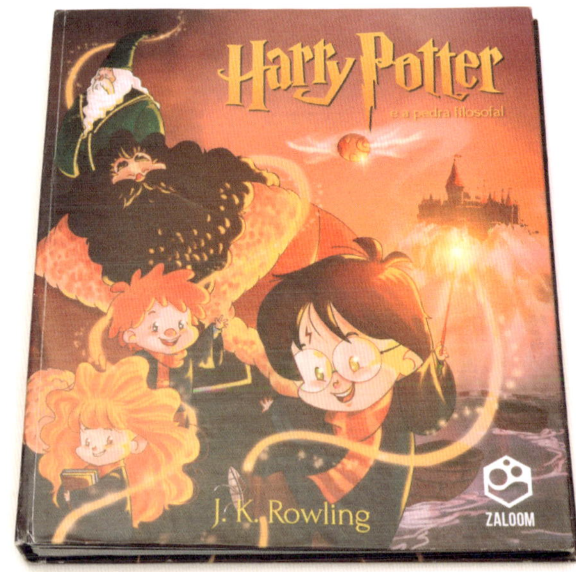

Grifinória
Coragem e Determinação

O verde dos jardins foi ficando branco de neve anunciando a chegada do Natal.

Hermione avisou os meninos que passaria o fim de ano com sua família e pediu para tomarem cuidado com Snape, pois acreditava que ele tinha ajudado o trasgo a entrar no castelo e enfeitiçado a vassoura de Harry.

Na manhã de Natal, Harry encontrou dois presentes ao lado de sua cama: um casaco, da mãe de Rony, e uma capa da invisibilidade, de alguém desconhecido. Ele a vestiu para passear a noite sem ser visto.

Em uma das salas que visitou havia um grande espelho, que para sua surpresa, refletia mais do que a sua imagem, mostrava o garoto feliz ao lado dos seus pais.

Harry passou horas imaginando se seria possível trazer seus pais de volta, até que a chegada de Dumbledore o assustou. O diretor explicou que o espelho mostrava apenas o desejo mais profundo do coração das pessoas e era impossível reviver os mortos.

Voltando as aulas, o trio começou a investigar Snape, pois desconfiava que ele estivesse planejando trazer Você-Sabe-Quem de volta. E Hermione, esperta como era, descobriu que ele procurava a Pedra Filosofal, capaz de dar a vida eterna a quem a usasse.

O único problema é que não faziam a mínima ideia de onde encontrá-la, ou de como impedir Snape de consegui-la. Por isso, decidiram procurar Hagrid, já que ele poderia saber de algo.

Chegando lá, o gigante falou mais do que devia, dizendo que eles não precisavam se preocupar, já que a Pedra estava muito bem escondida e protegida por um cachorro de três cabeças e vários outros feitiços.

Já era noite, quando ouviram um barulho estranho vindo do fogão, onde descobriram um ovo dentro de uma panela.

Hagrid colocou o ovo em cima da mesa e todos ficaram chocados ao vê-lo se quebrar e um lindo dragão sair de dentro dele.

[D]... contou aos amigos ... que aconteceu na flor...

Decididos a encontrar a Pedra Filosofal para impedir Snape, o trio passou a procurar no castelo o cachorro de três cabeças do qual Hagrid havia falado.

Harry, em um dos seus passeios noturnos com a capa da invisibilidade, encontrou no terceiro andar, o andar proibido, uma sala muito suspeita. O garoto jurava ter ouvido latidos vindos dela, mas não conseguiu passar pela porta que estava trancada.

Imaginando ser o monstro a quem Hagrid carinhosamente chamava de Fofo, o trio começou a pensar no que fazer para passar por ele.

Hermione não conhecia nenhum feitiço poderoso o bastante para derrubar o cão, por isso, foram conversar com Hagrid para tentar conseguir alguma informação.

Ao chegarem na cabana, encontraram o gigante triste pela partida de Norberto, o dragão que viram nascer. Hagrid lembrava do momento em que havia ganho o ovo no Caldeirão Furado de um desconhecido com o rosto coberto. Naquele dia, conversaram sobre como cuidar de animais imensos e como era simples fazê-los dormir com música.

Ouvindo a história Hermione juntou as informações e concluiu que poderia ser Snape o desconhecido no Caldeirão Furado. Se assim fosse, era possível que ele já soubesse como passar pelo Fofo.

Sem tempo, os três correram para o andar proibido. Hermione conseguiu abrir a porta usando um feitiço e lá dentro encontraram Fofo adormecido ao som de uma harpa.

O cachorro ocupava todo o espaço entre o teto e o piso. Tinha três cabeças e quatro patas imensas que protegiam uma porta no chão.

Quando caminhavam para o alçapão a harpa parou de tocar despertando o monstro. Assustados, correram para salvar suas vidas e pularam a tempo de entrar na porta antes que o cão conseguisse comê-los.

Por fim, eles tiveram aula
de voo em vassoura.
Harry aprendeu rápido,
foi o primeiro a voar
e por isso entrou para
o time da Grifinória.

GRINGOTES

Chegando lá, o gigante falou
mais do que devia, dizendo
que eles não precisavam se
preocupar, já que a Pedra estava
muito bem escondida e protegida
por um cachorro de três cabeças
e vários outros feitiços.

Já era noite, quando ouviram
um barulho estranho vindo
do fogão, onde descobriram
um ovo dentro de uma panela.

Hagrid colocou o ovo
em cima da mesa e todos
ficaram chocados ao vê-lo
se quebrar e um lindo dragão
sair de dentro dele.

Home
Made Home

Designer
Agata Królak

Material
**150gsm uncoated Munken
Print White paper**

Size
300mm x 400mm

Completion
2013

Publisher
Wydawnictwo Wytwórnia

'Home Made Home' (*Wytwórnik Domowy*) is a part of a series of activity books developed by Wydawnictwo Wytwórnia. The story takes on the themes of home and interior design and each spread is dedicated to one space in the house, such as the kitchen, bedroom, bathroom, and garden. As readers choose the wall color, set a dinner table, or arrange the pantry, the book encourages uninhibited fun and play. The designer, Agata Królak, felt it very important to leave as much space as possible for readers to be creative.

Bright colors and simple shapes evoke a childlike spirit and mixed-media illustrations are designed to stimulate activity and encourage experimentation with technique, texture, form, and color. The typography is intended to be friendly and easy to read and select words in bold and a larger font size teach home-themed vocabulary and emphasize the given task of each spread.

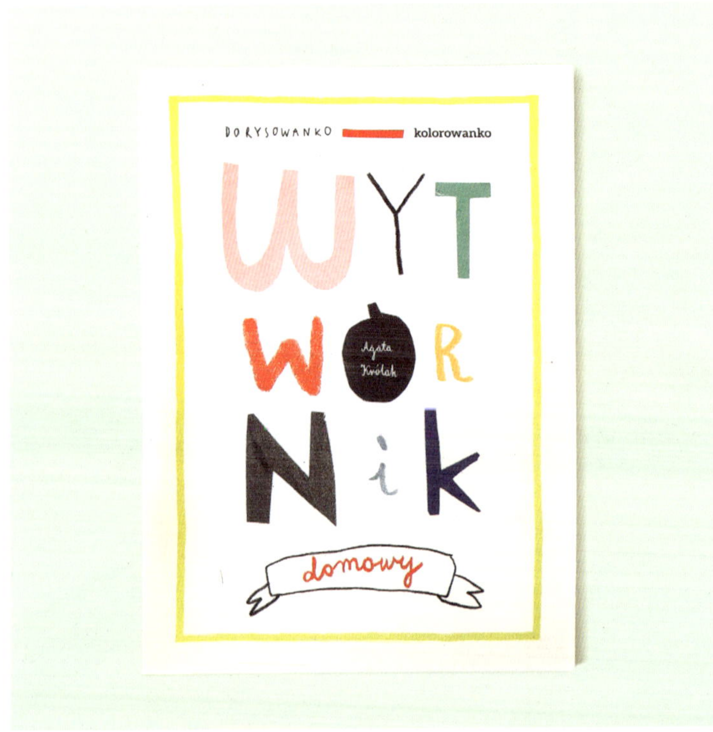

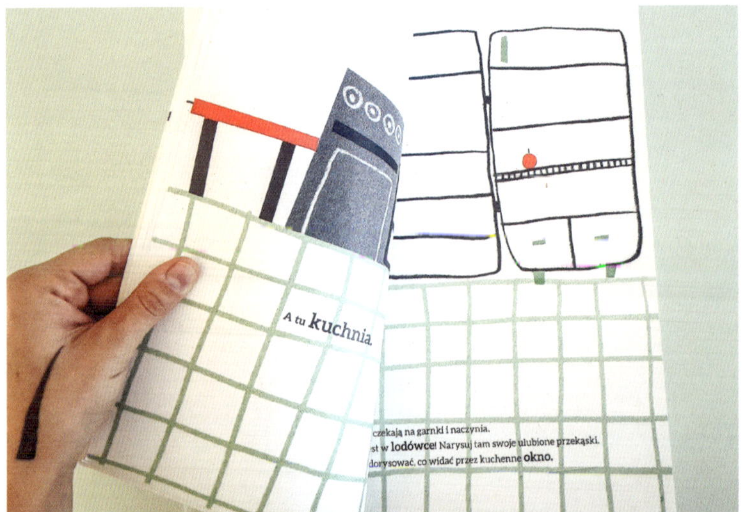

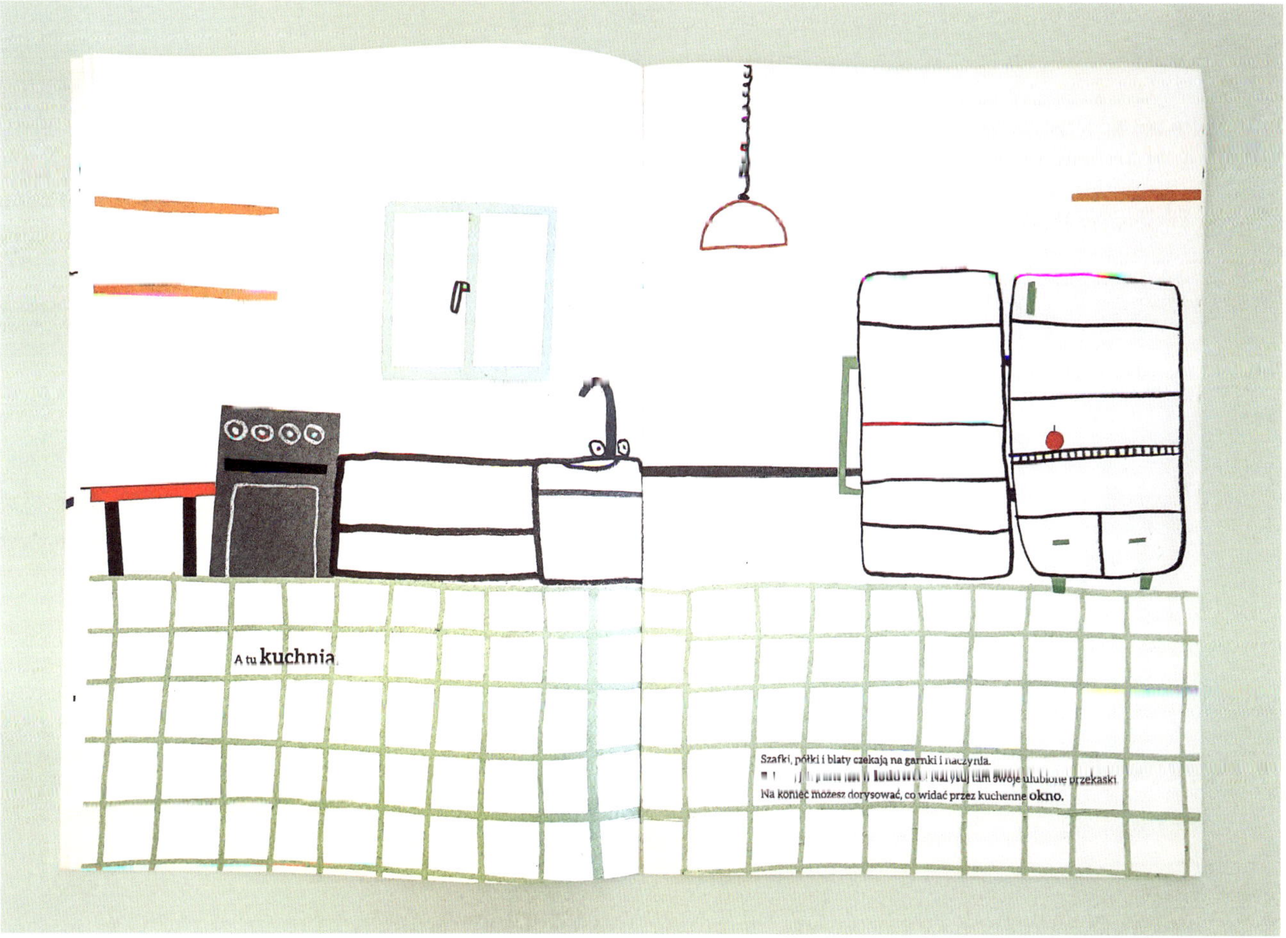

A tu **kuchnia**.

Szafki, półki i blaty czekają na garnki i naczynia.
[illegible] lodówce. Narysuj tam swoje ulubione przekąski.
Na koniec możesz dorysować, co widać przez kuchenne **okno**.

To jest **ogród**.

Narysuj **trawę i kwiaty**, a na drzewach – swoje ulubione **owoce**.
Możesz dorysować też **ścieżkę**, która prowadzi do domu.
A może ktoś mieszka w Twoim ogrodzie?

Experimental Study Book

Designers
Maria Turchaninova,
Madina Turchaninova

Size
147mm x 210mm

Completion
2015

The designers developed an interactive pop-up book for children to learn and play with each letter. The book is based on one of the designer's favorite fonts, Helvetica, and each letter plays a role in the story. The design is intended to surprise children at each turn of a page and children can explore and play interactively with each letter; for example, by spinning a wheel, pulling a tab, or dividing one letter into two. In this way, children can experiment with the shape of the letters to learn and memorize the alphabet.

Bramble Wood Activity Book

Designer
Sophie Corrigan

Material
**Matte paper,
textured paper,
shiny card**

Size
200mm x 200mm

Completion
2012

Sophie Corrigan created this full-color children's activity book based on a woodland theme. The designer used different interactive elements, materials, and drawing methods on each page. The design is simplistic, yet interactive, and the characters almost created themselves through the designer's experiments with media. A restricted color palette is achieved with a colorize feature on digital-editing software and the text is freehand for a spontaneous and playful feel.

The designer researched different ways to engage the reader and employed a method that would encourage their interaction with the artwork. In some cases readers need to complete or add an element to finish the artwork on a page.

i have...
big, googly
eyes,

soft wiggly
arms,

and jelly
legs that
hop.

i have...
big, googly
eyes,

big claws,

and large,
bouncy
legs.

i have...
long, floppy
ears,

cute little
paws,

and large,
bouncy
legs.

WOLF CAVE
grr...
ATTICUS
ATTICUS THE NAUGHTY WOLF WAS SO HUNGRY HE COULDN'T WAIT TO HUNT FOR FOOD!
PUNISH HIM BY COLOURING HIM IN YOUR LEAST FAVOURITE COLOUR!

DOG, FOX, OR WOLF?
YOU DECIDE, THEN COLOUR!

everyone will miss you... Visit again soon!
HOME

QUICK!!
DRAW SOMETHING
IN CELIA'S WAY,
TO STOP HER EATING
LIAM!
LIAM THE HARE
CELIA THE FOX

In the Woods

Designer
Lea Suijkerbuijk

Material
MDF, paper, birch

Size
220mm x 305mm

Completion
2014

In the Woods is a multifunctional book with illustrations and laser-cut wooden animals. Every spread features a different woodland scene in which the animals have multiple activities. Seven animals come in a wooden box with the book.

While each character has its own story, the dialogue and interactions between the world and animals come from the reader's imagination. This means the book can be experienced multiple times with new stories. The spreads can be combined to form a panoramic landscape, which serves as a playground for the stories. Possible future add-ons include a water world, cloud world, and desert.

Index

Published in Australia in 2016 by
The Images Publishing Group Pty Ltd
Shanghai Office
ABN 89 059 734 431
6 Bastow Place, Mulgrave, Victoria 3170, Australia
Tel: +61 3 9561 5544 Fax: +61 3 9561 4860
books@imagespublishing.com
www.imagespublishing.com

Title: Making Childhood Colorful: Designing Books for Children
Author: Wang Xiaodan
ISBN: 9781864706604

For Catalogue-in-Publication data, please see the National Library of Australia entry

Printed by Toppan Leefung Printing (Shenzhen) Co. Ltd / China